Layers of Learning
Year Four • Unit Five

Africa
Political Maps of the U.S.
Energy Conversion
Impressionism I

Published by HooDoo Publishing
United States of America
© 2017 Layers of Learning

(Grilled Cheese BTN Font) © Fontdiner - www.fontdiner.com
ISBN #978-1542980883

Units at a Glance: Topics For All Four Years of the Layers of Learning Program

1	History	Geography	Science	The Arts
1	Mesopotamia	Maps & Globes	Planets	Cave Paintings
2	Egypt	Map Keys	Stars	Egyptian Art
3	Europe	Global Grids	Earth & Moon	Crafts
4	Ancient Greece	Wonders	Satellites	Greek Art
5	Babylon	Mapping People	Humans in Space	Poetry
6	The Levant	Physical Earth	Laws of Motion	List Poems
7	Phoenicians	Oceans	Motion	Moral Stories
8	Assyrians	Deserts	Fluids	Rhythm
9	Persians	Arctic	Waves	Melody
10	Ancient China	Forests	Machines	Chinese Art
11	Early Japan	Mountains	States of Matter	Line & Shape
12	Arabia	Rivers & Lakes	Atoms	Color & Value
13	Ancient India	Grasslands	Elements	Texture & Form
14	Ancient Africa	Africa	Bonding	African Tales
15	First North Americans	North America	Salts	Creative Kids
16	Ancient South America	South America	Plants	South American Art
17	Celts	Europe	Flowering Plants	Jewelry
18	Roman Republic	Asia	Trees	Roman Art
19	Christianity	Australia & Oceania	Simple Plants	Instruments
20	Roman Empire	You Explore	Fungi	Composing Music

2	History	Geography	Science	The Arts
1	Byzantines	Turkey	Climate & Seasons	Byzantine Art
2	Barbarians	Ireland	Forecasting	Illumination
3	Islam	Arabian Peninsula	Clouds & Precipitation	Creative Kids
4	Vikings	Norway	Special Effects	Viking Art
5	Anglo Saxons	Britain	Wild Weather	King Arthur Tales
6	Charlemagne	France	Cells & DNA	Carolingian Art
7	Normans	Nigeria	Skeletons	Canterbury Tales
8	Feudal System	Germany	Muscles, Skin, Cardio	Gothic Art
9	Crusades	Balkans	Digestive & Senses	Religious Art
10	Burgundy, Venice, Spain	Switzerland	Nerves	Oil Paints
11	Wars of the Roses	Russia	Health	Minstrels & Plays
12	Eastern Europe	Hungary	Metals	Printmaking
13	African Kingdoms	Mali	Carbon Chemistry	Textiles
14	Asian Kingdoms	Southeast Asia	Non-metals	Vivid Language
15	Mongols	Caucasus	Gases	Fun With Poetry
16	Medieval China & Japan	China	Electricity	Asian Arts
17	Pacific Peoples	Micronesia	Circuits	Arts of the Islands
18	American Peoples	Canada	Technology	Indian Legends
19	The Renaissance	Italy	Magnetism	Renaissance Art I
20	Explorers	Caribbean Sea	Motors	Renaissance Art II

3	History	Geography	Science	The Arts
1	Age of Exploration	Argentina & Chile	Classification & Insects	Fairy Tales
2	The Ottoman Empire	Egypt & Libya	Reptiles & Amphibians	Poetry
3	Mogul Empire	Pakistan & Afghanistan	Fish	Mogul Arts
4	Reformation	Angola & Zambia	Birds	Reformation Art
5	Renaissance England	Tanzania & Kenya	Mammals & Primates	Shakespeare
6	Thirty Years' War	Spain	Sound	Baroque Music
7	The Dutch	Netherlands	Light & Optics	Baroque Art I
8	France	Indonesia	Bending Light	Baroque Art II
9	The Enlightenment	Korean Peninsula	Color	Art Journaling
10	Russia & Prussia	Central Asia	History of Science	Watercolors
11	Conquistadors	Baltic States	Igneous Rocks	Creative Kids
12	Settlers	Peru & Bolivia	Sedimentary Rocks	Native American Art
13	13 Colonies	Central America	Metamorphic Rocks	Settler Sayings
14	Slave Trade	Brazil	Gems & Minerals	Colonial Art
15	The South Pacific	Australasia	Fossils	Principles of Art
16	The British in India	India	Chemical Reactions	Classical Music
17	The Boston Tea Party	Japan	Reversible Reactions	Folk Music
18	Founding Fathers	Iran	Compounds & Solutions	Rococo
19	Declaring Independence	Samoa & Tonga	Oxidation & Reduction	Creative Crafts I
20	The American Revolution	South Africa	Acids & Bases	Creative Crafts II

4	History	Geography	Science	The Arts
1	American Government	USA	Heat & Temperature	Patriotic Music
2	Expanding Nation	Pacific States	Motors & Engines	Tall Tales
3	Industrial Revolution	U.S. Landscapes	Energy	Romantic Art I
4	Revolutions	Mountain West States	Energy Sources	Romantic Art II
5	Africa	U.S. Political Maps	Energy Conversion	Impressionism I
6	The West	Southwest States	Earth Structure	Impressionism II
7	Civil War	National Parks	Plate Tectonics	Post Impressionism
8	World War I	Plains States	Earthquakes	Expressionism
9	Totalitarianism	U.S. Economics	Volcanoes	Abstract Art
10	Great Depression	Heartland States	Mountain Building	Kinds of Art
11	World War II	Symbols & Landmarks	Chemistry of Air & Water	War Art
12	Modern East Asia	The South	Food Chemistry	Modern Art
13	India's Independence	People of America	Industry	Pop Art
14	Israel	Appalachian States	Chemistry of Farming	Modern Music
15	Cold War	U.S. Territories	Chemistry of Medicine	Free Verse
16	Vietnam War	Atlantic States	Food Chains	Photography
17	Latin America	New England States	Animal Groups	Latin American Art
18	Civil Rights	Home State Study I	Instincts	Theater & Film
19	Technology	Home State Study II	Habitats	Architecture
20	Terrorism	America in Review	Conservation	Creative Kids

Unit 4-5 Printable Pack

This unit includes printables at the end. To make life easier for you we also created digital printable packs for each unit. To retrieve your printable pack for Unit 4-5, please visit

www.layers-of-learning.com/digital-printable-packs/

Put the printable pack in your shopping cart and use this coupon code:

2617UNIT4-5

Your printable pack will be free.

Layers of Learning Introduction

This is part of a series of units in the Layers of Learning homeschool curriculum, including the subjects of history, geography, science, and the arts. Children from 1st through 12th can participate in the same curriculum at the same time - family school style.

The units are intended to be used in order as the basis of a complete curriculum (once you add in a systematic math, reading, and writing program). You begin with Year 1 Unit 1 no matter what ages your children are. Spend about 2 weeks on each unit. You pick and choose the activities within the unit that appeal to you and read the books from the book list that are available to you or find others on the same topic from your library. We highly recommend that you use the timeline in every history section as the backbone. Then flesh out your learning with reading and activities that highlight the topics you think are the most important.

Alternatively, you can use the units as activity ideas to supplement another curriculum in any order you wish. You can still use them with all ages of children at the same time.

When you've finished with Year One, move on to Year Two, Year Three, and Year Four. Then begin again with Year One and work your way through the years again. Now your children will be older, reading more involved books, and writing more in depth. When you have completed the sequence for the second time, you start again on it for the third and final time. If your student began with Layers of Learning in 1st grade and stayed with it all the way through she would go through the four year rotation three times, firmly cementing the information in her mind in ever increasing depth. At each level you should expect increasing amounts of outside reading and writing. High schoolers in particular should be reading extensively, and if possible, participating in discussion groups.

These icons will guide you in spotting activities and books that are appropriate for the age of child you are working with. But if you think an activity is too juvenile or too difficult for your kids, adjust accordingly. The icons are not there as rules, just guides.

☺ 1st-4th
☻ 5th-8th
☻ 9th-12th

Within each unit we share:

EXPLORATIONS, activities relating to the topic;
EXPERIMENTS, usually associated with science topics;
EXPEDITIONS, field trips;
EXPLANATIONS, teacher helps or educational philosophies.

In the sidebars we also include Additional Layers, Famous Folks, Fabulous Facts, On the Web, and other extra related topics that can take you off on tangents, exploring the world and your interests with a bit more freedom. The curriculum will always be there to pull you back on track when you're ready.

www.layers-of-learning.com

UNIT FIVE

AFRICA – POLITICAL MAPS – ENERGY CONVERSION - IMPRESSIONISM I

We need the tonic of wildness . . . at the same time that we are earnest to explore and learn all things, we require all things be mysterious and unexplorable . . . we can never have enough of nature.
-Henry David Thoreau

LIBRARY LIST

<table>
<tr>
<td rowspan="1">HISTORY</td>
<td>

Search for: African colonial period, South Africa history, Boers, Ethiopia history, King Leopold, David Livingstone, Cecil Rhodes, Victorian (this is the era in English history)

😊 😊 <u>African Princess: The Amazing Lives of Africa's Royal Women</u> by Joyce Hansen. Detailed portraits of African women from Queen Hatshepsut to the modern time.

😊 <u>The True Story of Cecil Rhodes in Africa</u> by Peter Gibbs. Out of print, look for used copies.

😊 <u>David Livingstone: Africa's Trailblazer</u> (Christian Heroes: Then & Now) by Janet Benge and Geoff Benge. Though written for a Christian audience, this book focuses more on the explorer than the missionary. Gives the reader a very good overview of the whole situation in Africa at this time period as well. Also look for "Mary Slessor" by the same authors.

😊 <u>Leopold II: Butcher of the Congo</u> by Tod Olson. Irreverent (but thorough) biography for kids.

😊 <u>At Her Majesty's Request: Story of an African Princess in Victorian England</u> by Walter Dean Meyers. A young African princess is about to be sacrificed by a rival tribe when an English captain persuades the king to give the girl as a gift to the White Queen (Victoria), saving her life. This is the true story of that young African girl.

😊 <u>Villainous Victorians</u> by Terry Deary. Focuses on what is going on in England at this time of African conquest.

😊 😊 <u>This Our Dark Country: The American Settlers of Liberia</u> by Catherine Reef.

😊 😊 <u>Armies of the Adowa Campaign 1896</u> by Sean McLachlan.

😊 😊 <u>Idi Amin</u> (Wicked History Series) by Steve Dougherty. Amin seized power in a bloody coup that plunged Uganda into decades of terror and poverty.

😊 <u>King Leopold's Ghost</u> by Adam Hochschild. Prepare to be horrified by the real life brutality in the Congo.

😊 <u>Heart of Darkness</u> by Joseph Conrad. Historical fiction of this time period.

😊 <u>Invictus</u>. This is an excellent movie about Nelson Mandela's attempts to unite the South African people through the sport of rugby following Apartheid. Rated PG-13.

😊 <u>Into Africa</u> by Martin Duggard. The story of Livingstone.

😊 <u>The Last Journals of David Livingstone, in Central Africa, from 1865 to His Death, Volume I: 1866-1868</u> by David Livingstone. Amazon has a free Kindle version.

😊 <u>Letters from Wankie: A Place in Colonial Africa</u> by Patricia Friedberg. A true story of a newly married young woman from London who followed her husband to South Africa where they lived in a remote colonial village in Africa in the 1950s.

</td>
</tr>
</table>

GEOGRAPHY	Search for: United States Maps, United States Atlas ☺ ☺ ☺ <u>Build a Giant Poster Coloring Book: United States Map</u> by Diana Zourelias. This is an intricate map with pictures of landmarks and landscape features. ☺ ☺ ☺ <u>The 50 States: Explore the U.S.A. With 50 Fact-Filled Maps</u> by Gabrielle Balkan and Sol Linero. ☺ ☺ <u>On the Map USA: A Workbook of U.S. Cities and States</u> by Education.com. Specifically for 3rd graders, but a range of ages could learn from it. ☺ ☺ <u>National Geographic Kids United States Atlas</u>. Get this especially if you plan on a road trip any time soon. ☺ ☺ <u>National Geographic Kids Ultimate Road Trip United States Atlas</u>. Choose from this one or the one above. This one includes puzzles and games along with the maps. ☺ ☺ <u>Rand McNally Road Atlas</u>. Get this if you will be doing any road trips this year. Your kids can practice reading a map as you go. They make a new one each year so be sure you get an up-to-date version.
SCIENCE	Search for: energy conversion, energy transformation, energy, potential energy, kinetic energy, collisions (physics) ☺ ☺ <u>Janice Van Cleave's Energy For Every Kid</u> by Janice Van Cleave. Lots of simple experiments about energy. ☺ ☺ <u>The Powerful World of Energy with Max Axiom, Super Scientist</u> by Agnieszka Biskup. Graphic novel format. ☺ ☺ <u>Energy</u> by Chris Woodford. From DK, this is a beautiful book. ☺ <u>Basic Physics: A Self Teaching Guide</u> by Karl F. Khun. Read or review chapter 3. ☺ <u>CK-12 Basic Physics</u>. This is free on Kindle. Read the chapter on energy. It briefly explains the concepts and the math and then has a set of practice problems.
THE ARTS	Search for: Impressionism ☺ ☺ ☺ <u>Impressionism: 50 Paintings You Should Know</u> by Ines Janet Engelmann. A great place to begin learning about the Impressionists. ☺ ☺ ☺ <u>Impressionist Art Masterpieces to Color</u> by Marty Noble. ☺ ☺ ☺ <u>The Impressionists</u> by Franscesco Salvi. This book pairs the history of France with the Impressionist movement. It is full of interesting information, but is illustrated, so it's great for all ages. ☺ ☺ ☺ <u>Impressionism</u> by Jude Welton. A DK Eyewitness book. Shows beautiful versions of the most famous paintings with excellent explanations. ☺ <u>Katie and the Impressionists</u> by James Mayhew. Your child gets to explore several impressionists paintings with the heroine of the book, a girl named Katie. ☺ <u>Phillipe in Monet's Garden</u> by Lisa Jobe Carmack. A frog escapes the frog catchers and finds refuge in Monet's garden. ☺ ☺ <u>Impressionism: 13 Artists Children Should Know</u> by Florian Heine. ☺ ☺ <u>Impressionism</u> by Peggy J. Parks.

HISTORY: AFRICA

Fabulous Fact

Most historians consider the Berlin Conference of 1884 as the starting point for the Scramble for Africa. The conference was held so that European powers could divide up Africa without having to go to war over it.

Austria-Hungary, Belgium, Denmark, France, the UK, Italy, Netherlands, Portugal, Germany, Spain, Sweden-Norway, Ottoman Empire, and the United States all attended the conference.

Famous Folks

Joseph Conrad was a Polish-British writer who traveled up the Congo in the 1890s as part of a steamer crew. Later he wrote a book called *Heart of Darkness* based on his experiences.

His book questions imperialism, racism, and what it means to be a "savage." He draws parallels between the savages of the Congo and the savages of London.

Africa was colonized later than the rest of the world. For centuries the Europeans had been content with merely buying and selling thousands of Africans across the sea to the Americas. Africa was called the "dark continent" because, aside from a few ports and the basic shape of the coastline, the Europeans knew nothing of the interior of Africa. But the European powers were constantly vying for power over one another, and colonies and wealth were two ways of keeping score. Soon Africa became desirable, and European powers such as France, England, Portugal, Belgium, Italy, Germany, and Spain were colonizing and controlling vast sections, until in a very short time nearly all of Africa was governed by Europeans. The struggle between the European powers to gain land in Africa became known as the "Scramble for Africa."

It wasn't quite as simple as Europeans just wanting new land though. There were other factors involved. By the 1880s slavery had been eradicated throughout the western world. No European nations engaged in the African slave trade and slavery had been well established as a moral evil, but the slave trade within Africa was still alive and well. African chiefs still raided neighbors for the purpose of capturing slaves to sell to the Arab slave traders who came from the east or crossed the Sahara for their human cargo, and Africans still enslaved one another. Abolitionists in Britain felt strongly that slavery should be eradicated everywhere, not just in western nations, so there was a great deal of pressure for England to get involved.

Europeans, especially the British, also had an insatiable appetite for knowledge, scientific and geographic, of the whole planet. The Royal Geographical Society of London had been founded in 1830 and was actively training explorers in map making, latitude and longitude skills, drawing, and survival skills in the pure pursuit of knowledge. As they explored Africa and discovered its many natural resources, there were bound to be some who wanted to exploit those resources and gather wealth. New technology, such as shallow draft steam ships, made exploration up African rivers possible, extending the reach of Europeans. Also, diseases that previously had caused high mortality among uninitiated Europeans had been cured, allowing for not only more exploration, but also colonization and the formation of permanent forts and trade stations.

Henry Morton Stanley, an American, had been commissioned by King Leopold of Belgium to negotiate treaties with tribes and kingdoms along the Congo, setting off a race among European nations to get agreements on paper before anyone else.

The end of the slave trade also left a void which the free trade markets of Europe hurried to fill by creating markets for European manufactured goods and the newly discovered African raw resources such as gum, gold, diamonds, tin, coffee, sugar, palm oil, and salt. European markets had never quite believed Adam Smith when he spoke of free trade between nations. They still thought that exclusive control, or monopolies, was the way to greatest wealth. After all, freedom can be counterintuitive. Monopolies meant not only trading, but controlling colonies politically and militarily so that no one else could trade there.

😊 😊 😊 EXPLORATION: Timeline

Printable timeline squares can be found at the end of this unit.

- 1652 Dutch colonize the Cape of Good Hope as a weigh station for ships sailing to India
- 1806 England takes Cape Colony from Dutch, as part of Napoleonic Wars
- 1816 Shaka becomes king of the Zulus and systematically conquers all of his neighbors, depopulating southern Africa in the process
- 1836-1845 Great Trek
- 1838 Boers defeat the Zulus in battle
- 1841 David Livingstone begins to explore Africa
- 1879 Zulus are defeated by British
- 1880 French make a treaty turning the land north of the Congo into a French protectorate.
- 1881 Tunisia becomes a French protectorate
- 1882 British take sole rule of Egypt when the French pull out
- 1882 Italy takes control of Eritrea
- 1884 European nations make treaties dividing Africa
- 1885 Congo Free State established by Leopold II
- 1896 Italy defeated by Ethiopia at the Battle of Adwa
- 1902 British defeat the Boers in South Africa
- 1904-05 Herero of Namibia rise up against German overlords
- 1905 Maji-Maji rebel against German rule in East Africa
- 1912 Zulus unite to become the South African National Congress, which becomes the African National Congress (ANC)

😊 😊 😊 EXPLORATION: Shaka Zulu

Shaka was the illegitimate son of the king of the Zulus. He was exiled with his mother but taken in by a neighboring chief. He became a noted and great warrior in his early years, slowly gaining trust and power as a war leader. In spite of his prowess as a warrior and military commander, he preferred to use diplomacy

Fabulous Fact

Germany only became a unified nation in 1870 after the Franco-Prussian War. It had no colonies or real power within Europe. By 1880, Germany was wanting to expand its sphere of influence and grow its power and wealth. This greatly concerned both England and France. The German acquisition of colonies was part of the impetus for the Berlin Conference.

Germany's aggression in acquiring colonies and power and England's and France's desire to stop it from doing so would eventually break out in war in 1914.

On the Web

This student made video is a good introduction to African Colonialism: https://www.youtube.com/watch?v=AKJKEI-zaEpU

On the Web

Watch this video, the first of four, about Shaka Zulu: https://www.youtube.com/watch?v=BZL-GKFWlRzY

It does a great job of explaining why Shaka Zulu was so significant in the history of South Africa.

Fabulous Fact

Shaka transformed his people from a peaceful pastoral society to a war-like conquering empire.

Here is a picture, draw by Robert Baden Powell of Boy Scout fame, of a Zulu warrior.

Additional Layer

Africa before colonization:

There were a few European colonies on the coasts and thousands of different tribes in the interior. It only took 30 years to subdue the whole continent.

Map by davidjl123 / Somebody500, CC license, Wikimedia.

to get what he wanted - most of the time. After Shaka's father died, one of Shaka's brother's became the new ruler. But Shaka had him assassinated and assumed power. Under his leadership the Zulu tribe became more warlike and they routinely crushed their rival neighbors when those neighbors would not submit to diplomatic hegemony. Over time Shaka built a powerful empire in South Africa. In doing this, many thousands lost their lives in battles and massacres, and hundreds of thousands were displaced as they fled Shaka's armies.

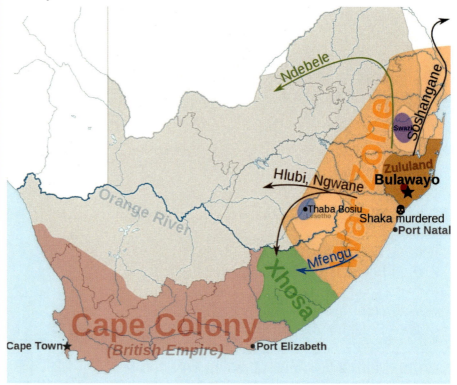

This map shows the extent of Shaka's empire. The Zulu tribe began in the dark orange area and expanded to the lighter orange regions. The arrows show the migrations of tribes who fled the Zulu armies. Map by Discott and shared under CC license on Wikimedia.

The Zulus fought with spears and hide shields. Shaka favored the short stabbing spear over the long throwing spear and taught his warriors close combat techniques. The shields were made of heavy cowhide and were used to open an enemy's defenses and then take advantage of the opening to stab him. The shields were issued by the king and remained his property. Different painted designs on the shields designated to which military unit a warrior belonged.

Shaka wanted his warriors to be the best, strongest, fastest, and toughest anywhere. He took away their sandals and made them travel and fight barefooted. He forced them to march over long distances, some even say as far as 50 miles in a single day, to toughen them up. He enlisted young children to train with the army. Insubordination was met with death.

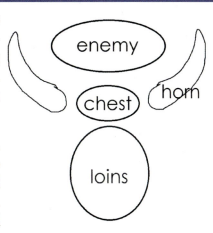

Shaka also created the bull tactic. The troops would be divided into three parts. The "chest" of the bull would directly attack the enemy. Then two "horns" would extend around and surround the enemy. Finally, the "loins" of the bull would lie in wait and be sent to wherever the main troops needed reinforcing.

Ten years into his reign Shaka was assassinated by another of his brothers.

During Shaka's reign the Europeans were still weak and eager to make treaties with the African tribes. They had some treaties with Shaka, but, on the whole, Shaka dismissed them as unimportant and their weapons as overrated. It wouldn't be until several decades after Shaka's death that war would break out between the Zulus and the British.

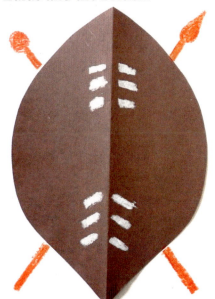

Make a Zulu war shield out of construction paper. Begin with tan or brown paper to simulate the color of the hides. Then use oil pastels or paints to make designs on the shields.

Glue the shield to a piece of background paper and then draw on crossed spears behind the shield. You can glue down only one edge of the shield and write facts about the Zulus or draw a map of their empire behind the shield.

☺ ☺ ☺ **EXPLORATION: Great Trek**

Way back in 1652 the Dutch had established a city on the tip of South Africa called Cape Town, which was primarily a stop over for ships traveling in the spice trade to India and beyond. But many Dutch individuals, French Huguenots, and Germans also wanted more land and more freedom. They moved to the area

Explanation

Back in Unit 3-7 we talked about the "black legend" in connection with Spain and its colonies. The black legend is also a problem when talking about Colonial Africa.

People have very strong feelings about the colonization of Africa, the continuing influence of the west in Africa, and the history and value of Africa in general. This causes them to paint all Europeans as evil, bloodthirsty, selfish, greedy, conquerors. While there were some very dark and evil actions and individuals involved in the colonization of Africa, the truth is that most Europeans, (average people and even many politicians), had been lied to about Africa or were strongly opposed to what was happening there. In addition, not everything the Europeans did in Africa was bad. Likewise, not everything about the native Africans was virtuous.

The important thing in education is to present actual facts from many points of view and then help kids arrive at their own conclusions. We encourage you to use many different sources and hold discussions.

On the Web

It is the popular thing to universally condemn the Boers because they fought against the natives and practiced slavery. But there was quite a bit more to their story than all that. Read this account: http://public.wsu.edu/~campbelld/crane/great.htm.

Fabulous Fact

The Battle of Blood River was fought after one of the Boer leaders, Piet Retif, and his entourage were massacred during peace talks with the Zulus. The Boers determined to revenge the deaths and bring the Zulus to heel. 470 Boers fought with guns from the protection of their wagon circle while 15,000 Zulu warriors attacked with spears and cow hide shields. After the battle the Boers had not lost a single man, but the Zulus had lost 3,000. The Zulu nation descended into civil war. The Boers established their settlement.

around Cape Town and formed their own independent nation of freemen. In 1806 the British took Cape Town and put the Boers, as the Dutch settlers were called, under their control. "Boer" means farmer in their language. The Boers did not like the way the British ruled. They protested against it but got nowhere, so they decided to move. They took their households and families and trekked north and east to new fertile lands, held at the time by the Zulus and other tribes. This migration, from 1835 to 1854, is called the Great Trek. The Boers fought the natives in bitter and bloody battles, finally defeating them in 1838. The Boers established three new free nations called Transvaal, Natal, and the Orange Free State.

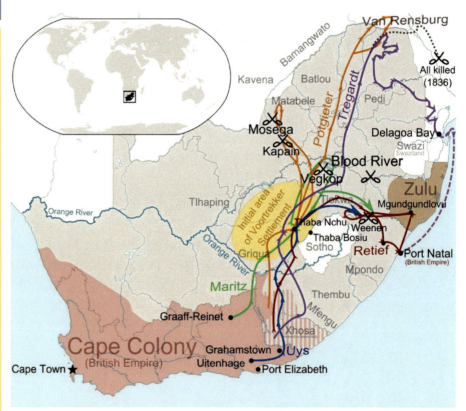

This map shows the routes of a few of the major wagon trains. Their routes took them straight into the path of the Zulus and war. Map by Discott and shared under CC license on Wikimedia.

The Great Trek expanded the area of European control in South Africa and made a power shift among the tribes as they allied and attacked and were defeated by the Boers.

One of the things that made the Boers successful in battle was the formation of the laager, a circle of wagons arranged for defense. The Boers could fire their guns from protected positions while the Zulus, using short stabbing spears, were lacking even projectile weapons. It meant that small numbers of Boers could defeat forces many times their own strength.

At the end of this unit is a covered wagon printable. Make several copies on card stock. Cut out the wagons, color them, and glue them into a circle, a laager. Draw your own paper Trekker figures to add to your scene. The people included children, women, men, and black servants of all ages and sexes.

😊 😊 EXPLORATION: Boer War

After the Boers became established in new colonies, gold was discovered in 1866 in the Orange Free State. Gold hunters flocked to the Orange Free State and then Transvaal as gold was discovered there as well. In 1867 diamonds were also discovered. The new settlers were mostly British from Cape Colony. These new settlers wanted British rule, and several uprisings and protests were formed. The governments of the two Boer Republics finally declared war on Britain in 1899 as the British tried to overthrow the republics. The British thought they could easily subdue these farmers in a few months, but the Boers held out for years. Eventually Britain did prevail, and in 1902 the Orange Free State and Transvaal came under British rule. As part of the treaty the united states were promised self-rule. In 1910 the British formed the state of South Africa, fulfilling this promise.

The Boer War was exceptionally brutal. The Boers, desperate, engaged in guerrilla warfare against the British. The British retliated and engaged in scorched earth policies, burning out civilians, sewing farmers' fields with salt, and rounding up all the women and children in concentration camps where 26,000 would die of starvation, exposure, and disease.

Watch this ten minute video about the Boer War: https://www.youtube.com/watch?v=0_7yNjQquik (Disturbing, please preview).

At the end of this unit you will find a printable map showing the four European nations of southern Africa in 1900. They were Cape Colony, Natal, Transvaal, and Orange Free State. Decorate the map using crayons, colored pencils or pens. These are the states that the British united through the Boer War to become the nation of South Africa.

Additional Layers

Germany owned four colonies in Africa: German East Africa (Tanzania), Togo, German South-West Africa (Namibia), and Cameroon.

During their reign two major uprisings took place: the Herero Wars in German South-West Africa and the Maji Maji Rebellion in German East Africa.

Famous Folks

Carl Peters was a German colonist who was essential in the establishment of German East-Africa (Tanzania). He treated the native population brutally and exploited them shamelessly, believing them to be of an inferior race. He was punished for his actions back in Germany and removed from office, but not before he had been responsible for many thousands of deaths and several uprisings.

Fabulous Fact

Apartheid is an Afrikaans word meaning "apartness." The idea was that the races would flourish if kept separate.

Deep Thoughts

The primary cause of apartheid was fear. White people were afraid of losing their culture, identity, and power. They thought that if they gave blacks equal rights and respect that blacks would take over their country. They thought if blacks took over, the whites would become the oppressed group.

Famous Folks

Hendrik Verwoerd was the first Boer prime minister of South Africa and the architect of apartheid.

He was assassinated in 1966.

Fabulous Fact

Most of the people who protested the apartheid laws were blacks or mixed races, but about 20% of the white population also opposed apartheid. The most famous group of white protesters were the Black Sashes, a group of white South African women who wore black sashes everywhere they went in mourning for the loss of rule of law. Internationally, apartheid was condemned with trade, diplomatic, and sports embargoes against the country.

☺ ☺ EXPLORATION: Apartheid

Not all of the Boers were content with British rule. They expressed their rebellion by creating political parties to take over the government. The Boers were Christians who thought the Bible mandated the white race as superior to other races. They used the Bible as an excuse for the political oppression of the black Africans in South Africa, including slavery, denial of the vote, harsh property laws, required use of passes and restriction of movement, and unequal access to resources such as education and medicine. Apartheid was not just a way of thinking, it was the official policy of the Boer government that was swept into power in South Africa in 1948. The National Party (Boer government) gave the set of segregationist laws a name: apartheid.

Watch this short video about apartheid: https://www.youtube.com/watch?v=2f2k6iDFCL4.

Many people protested the apartheid laws with demonstrations, sit-ins, newspaper editorials, newsletter campaigns, and marches. Other times the protests were violent. Factories, businesses, and individuals were physically attacked. Terrorist measures like bombings in public places were aimed at civilians. The organizations behind the protests were the African National Congress (ANC), Pan Africanist Congress (PAC), and other smaller groups.

Many protesters were imprisoned for days, weeks, or even years. In several instances police and military met protesters with deadly force, such as in the Sharpeville Massacre of 1960. In addition, the South African government supported independent paramilitary groups that carried out assassinations and attacks on ANC and PAC members in South Africa and around the world.

Finally, in 1994, the vote was extended to all adults in South Africa and a new government led by the ANC came into power. Nelson Mandela became the president of South Africa and apartheid was officially ended.

Divide a sheet of paper into four equal quadrants. Label the quadrants "laws," "protests & protesters,"

Apartheid

laws	protests & protestors

- forced removals to segregated towns/neighborhoods
 	
- passes required to move or work
 	
- loss of citizenship & voting rights
 	
- segregated schools, hospitals, restaurants, bathrooms, buses, beaches, stores, theaters, etc.
 	
- no intermarriage between races
	- African National Congress (ANC)
	  - communist
	  - peaceful & terrorist tactics

enforcement	resolution

"enforcement," and "resolution." As you read more about apartheid fill in the quadrants with information about these four topics relating to apartheid.

☺ ☻ EXPLORATION: Dr. Livingstone, I Presume

David Livingstone was a Scottish congregationalist missionary and doctor who went to Africa before it had been explored or penetrated by Europeans in order to preach and teach and serve in Africa. He was an ardent abolitionist and believed that the way to stop the slave trade, which was still very much alive in Africa in the mid 1800's, was to educate, convert, and enlighten the Africans who would then stop slavery on their own. He did not go to Africa out of curiosity or to exploit it; he went to save it.

In the process, this heroic explorer who was undaunted by disease, native aggression, or the enormity of his single handed task, became a folk hero to the English-speaking world and most of Europe. Read more about him and his story: www.livingstoneonline.org.

Make a set of explorer binoculars. You need two toilet paper tubes, card stock or construction paper, and fancy supplies to decorate with: sequins, glitter, stickers, whatever you would like.

1. Cover each tube with the paper of your choice,
2. Make a bridge of paper to connect the two tubes together.
3. Decorate your binoculars.
4. Attach a piece of string or yarn for a neck strap.

As you build the binoculars, talk about David Livingstone's life

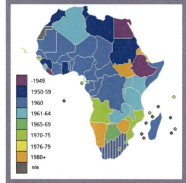

Famous Folks

Mary Slessor was born in 1848 in Scotland to a mother who desired above all to have a son who went out and preached as a missionary, but it was not to be, as all of her little boys died in childhood.

Mary, however, heard about the death of David Livingstone when she was 27 and determined to go to Africa and serve as he had. She lived there until she died at the age of 66, having endured and dared every bit as much, if not more, than the great Livingstone himself. She saved hundreds of African babies from infanticide, raising several of them herself and formally adopting one.

Additional Layer

From 1980 to 2003 Liberia experienced a bloody civil war, reducing it from economic prosperity to poverty. Learn more.

and his goals. He worked hard to serve and bring knowledge to people who were in darkness. Encourage your kids to look out (with their binoculars) for people who might need their help and to serve others.

😊 😊 😊 EXPLORATION: Map of African Colonies

In 1884, several major European countries met in Berlin to decide who got what part of Africa. The results can be seen in the "Scramble for Africa" map which you will find at the end of this unit. Make copies of the map and color the key and the regions on the map to match.

The only two countries to remain independent were Liberia and Ethiopia. Liberia had been founded by the United States as a homeland for all freed African slaves who desired to return to Africa and so was off limits to Europe. Ethiopia was Christian (and had been since the earliest days of Christianity) and already had diplomatic agreements and alliances with European nations, but more importantly, Ethiopia militarily defeated Italy when they tried to take the country by force.

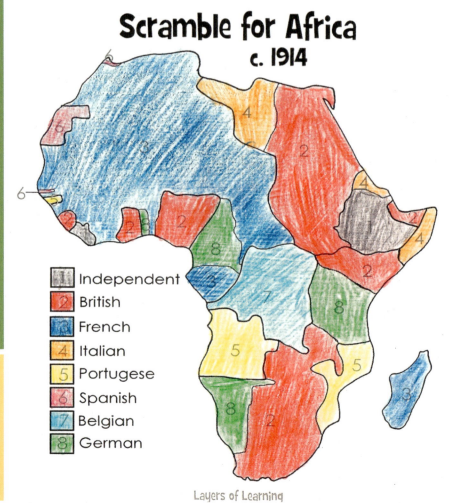

Scramble for Africa c. 1914

1	Independent
2	British
3	French
4	Italian
5	Portugese
6	Spanish
7	Belgian
8	German

Layers of Learning

☺ ☺ ☺ EXPLORATION: Cecil Rhodes

Cecil Rhodes was born in Britain in 1853. At the age of 18 he was sent to South Africa to live with his brother because his parents feared for his health. A year after arriving in Natal his brother's farm had failed and the two boys went to Cape Colony. With financial backing, they began buying up small, failing diamond mines. The mines began to turn a profit, and the Rhodes brothers bought up more and more mines, eventually owning a worldwide monopoly on diamonds.

In 1880, Cecil ran for parliament of Cape Colony and won a seat. In 1888, he founded the De Beers Diamond Company, which was named after a previous owner of one of the larger mines. By 1890, his wealth and influence were great enough that he was elected Prime Minister of Cape Colony. His policies included British imperialism. He believed the Anglo-Saxon race was superior to all others and that England ought to rule the world for the benefit of everyone. He used his political and financial influence to convince the London parliament to give his British South Africa Company the governance of newly colonized lands north of Cape Colony. This land was named Rhodesia, and the prime economic activity was in mines owned by Rhodes. His imperialism also led him to attempt the overthrow of the Dutch nation of Transvaal in 1896. This action eventually led to the Boer War. While Prime Minister, he also championed the building of a telegraph and railroad that would stretch from Cairo to Cape Town, making British rule of Africa possible. This dream was never realized. Rhodes died in 1902 at the age of 48.

Make a paper puppet of Cecil Rhodes dressed in military khakis. While you work, talk about the life of Cecil Rhodes and how he influenced Africa. Talk about imperialism and Rhodes' attitude about the capacity of native people for good government.

Additional Layer

What if the Scramble for Africa had never happened? This video explores what might have happened in Africa if the Europeans had only traded with, but not conquered, the Africans. https://www.youtube.com/watch?v=FnN0Ru-rtJWc

What do you think might have happened?

Additional Layer

One of the biggest problems in Africa today is the shape of the borders between countries. Read this: http://freakonomics.com/2011/12/01/the-violent-legacy-of-africas-arbitrary-borders/

Writer's Workshop

We can't go back in time and fix African colonialism. So why bother learning about it? What does learning about this time period really teach you? What is happening in current events or perhaps in your personal life that you could apply the lessons from this time period to? What can be done about Africa, its poverty, and instability going forward?

Write an essay answering some of these questions.

Famous Folks

Henry Morton Stanley was born Welsh and abandoned by his mother soon after birth. He grew up passed between relatives until he ended up in a workhouse at a very young age.

As a young man he immigrated to the United States just in time to join the Civil War.

After the war he traveled to Africa on an expedition to find both the famous explorer David Livingstone and the source of the Nile. On another expedition he explored and mapped the Congo. He was hired by King Leopold of Belgium to make treaties with natives along the Congo and claim the land for Leopold.

Fabulous Fact

The soldiers of the Force Publique were Africans from various areas attracted by the wages. The officers were all Belgians. The soldiers were brutal.

Now that Africa is self governing, do you think Rhodes was right or wrong? Was Africa better under British rule, or better off on its own? You may want to especially look at the history of Zimbabwe, which was part of the land governed by Rhodes' company. On the back of the puppet write down your thoughts about Rhodes and Imperialism.

☺ ☺ ☺ EXPLORATION: King Leopold II

Leopold became king of Belgium in 1865 at the age of 30. He believed that in order to make Belgium great it needed overseas colonies. But Leopold was subject to the parliament of Belgium, which did not agree with him and could not afford the acquisition of colonies anyway. So, in 1876, Leopold formed a private company whose aim was, on the surface, to explore and map the unexplored. The real aim of the company was to acquire territory through conquest. Leopold controlled this private company utterly. He hired Henry Morton Stanley, an American, to explore and establish a colony in the Congo. In 1884 and 1885 the

This is a missionary to the Congo holding up the arm of a young boy who has had his hand cut off by the Force Publique. The missionaries spoke out in spite of being threated by Leopold and his mercenaries.

European powers and the United States met in Berlin to negotiate over who would own what in Africa. King Leopold's claim to the Congo was upheld and Leopold became the absolute ruler in the Congo, without the aid of any parliament. He hired a private mercenary army, the Force Publique, to enforce his rule.

The natural resources of the Congo, including ivory and rubber, were exploited and the natives enslaved to harvest the resources. Foreigners were restricted from entering the country in order to hide the atrocities committed by Leopold's private army. If any resistance was attempted or if harvest quotas were not met, the retribution was terrible. People were beaten, mutilated, and killed for the most minor of infractions or merely as an example to the others. An estimated one half of the total population died, approximately 10 million, as a result of exhaustion, mistreatment, malnutrition, disease resulting from mistreatment, or executions.

Eventually the truth of what was happening in the Congo leaked out, mostly through missionaries who had braved the wrath of Leopold to investigate. In 1904 the British commissioned an official investigation. What they found horrified the world. Writers like Mark Twain and Sir Arthur Conan Doyle spoke out against the abuses. But it wasn't until 1908 that the Belgian parliament finally succeeded in wresting control of the Congo from Leopold.

In 1960, the Democratic Republic of the Congo became independent. Since then the country has been plagued with unrest, military coups, civil wars, rampant human rights abuses, and governmental corruption.

Find the Democratic Republic of the Congo on a modern globe or map. This country was formerly King Leopold's colony.

Masks have always been an important part of Congo culture. They are especially used in religious dances. Make a mask from a paper plate and tissue paper. Cut out holes for eyes. Paint the paper plate. After the paint is dry decorate it further with beads, colored paper, oil pastels, or feathers. Glue colorful strips of tissue paper or raffia sticking out around the rim of the mask. We made ours with yellow, red, and turquoise blue because those are the colors of the flag of the Democratic Republic of the Congo.

While you work, talk about King Leopold, what he did, and how

Additional Layer

The 1994 Rwandan genocide is an example of the chaos that Africa is still experiencing. Learn more about the Rwandan genocide. Is that event tied to colonialism? How?

Additional Layer

When Belgium pulled out of the Congo in 1960, they had so destroyed the fabric of society that virtually no one was educated. Family and tribal groups were no longer intact. The previous native government structures were completely destroyed. The native belief systems, history, and heritage were eradicated. All of the government, health care, and education systems were run by white Belgians, who left en masse upon independence. In essence, they left the Congo in a state of anarchy.

The Congo is probably the most extreme example of the unmitigated damage Europeans did to an African nation, but similar things happened all over Africa.

This man explains some of the aftermath within Africa: https://www.youtube.com/watch?v=h-wOqmThOLoU.

Additional Layer

Read more about the history of the Democratic Republic of the Congo since 1960.

How do you think the experience of the Congo under the Belgians has contributed to the unrest since independence? Is the unrest proof that the Congo cannot rule itself?

What could the Belgians have done to prepare the colony for the modern world and ensure peaceful and productive rule?

Famous Folks

Haile Selassie was the ruler of Ethiopia from 1916 to 1974. He guided his people through two world wars and modernization but was deposed in a coup d'etat in 1974.

After his rule ended there was a lot of unrest in Ethiopia.

Library List

See if your library has the 1999 documentary film *Adwa: An African Victory* by director Haile Gerima.

his actions were wrong. Talk about the culture of the Congo and how its people are still suffering from the effects of the abuses they suffered under. The mask you made represents the value, spirit, and hope of the people of Congo.

😊 😊 😊 EXPLORATION: The Battle of Adwa

The Europeans didn't always have things their own way. Most of Africa was backward, war-torn, decimated by the slave trade, and crippled by their own superstitions, but not Ethiopia. It had been a center of learning since ancient times. In 1896, Ethiopia was invaded by Italy which wished to make Ethiopia a colony. Italy had first tried to make Ethiopia a vassal state through diplomatic trickery, but the King of Ethiopia, Menelik, caught on quickly and refused, so Italy decided force of arms was in order. Menelik's forces were riflemen and lancers who outnumbered the already demoralized and homesick Italian troops by an estimated five or six times.

The Italians blundered repeatedly, using their older rifles and cartridges in a fit of false economy. They misunderstood the terrain and made an overly complicated battle plan. Meanwhile, Menelik waited patiently for the Italians to show up and then soundly routed them, sending them running back home, abandoning their artillery and baggage trains. He had eliminated the Italian threat in Ethiopia and secured independence for Ethiopia for another generation. Ethiopia's success became a rallying point for African pride and independence movements in the 20th century.

See the lady on the horse with the big revolver in the lower left of

the painting? That's Empress Taitu who said "I am a woman. I do not like war. However, I would rather die than accept your deal."

The Ethiopians knew the war was about more than politics and power struggles; it was a moral battle. Should a people have self-determination and freedom, or should the spoils go to the strongest? Do we believe in the right of conquest or not? The Ethiopians did not; they thought they ought to rule themselves and were willing to die for that belief. They inspired all of Africa.

To highlight their moral ground we can look at the aftermath of the battle. The Italians had turned tail and run from the battle without weapons, food, horses, or their general. But the Ethiopians just let them go. They could have followed and wiped out every last man, but they did not fight the battle to kill Italians. Menelik could have easily annexed the neighboring Italian lands in Eritrea, but he did not fight the battle to gain land and power. Ethiopia fought the battle to preserve their independence. Menelik immediately signed a new treaty with Italy, demanding no reparations, but asking only peace.

The Ethiopian flag with the colors of green, yellow, and red became an African symbol of independence, and many African countries and countries with African heritage, like Jamaica, have adopted those colors on their flags as well.

Find an interesting stick from outside. Clean all the bark off of it . Paint it completely with white spray paint. Let the paint dry. Then use brushes and acrylic paints to paint yellow, red, and green designs on the stick. Add yarn or raffia for decoration. This stick represents the triumph of the Battle of Adwa and the independence of Africa.

On the Web

Read all about it! Italy's Terrible Defeat!

http://query.nytimes.com/mem/archive-free/pdf?res=9806EED-E1738E233A25757C0A-9659C94679ED7CF

Check out the archived copy of the New York Times article about the Battle of Adwa from March 4, 1896.

Additional Layer

African nations since independence have been interfered with repeatedly by western powers. The U.S. staged several coups, armed rebels, and assassinated presidents, sending nations like the D.R. Congo into civil war repeatedly. The U.S.S.R. behaved similarly. They used Africa in their Cold War power struggles. Decades of this on the heels of colonialism has made it difficult for Africa to be able to stabilize. Learn more.

Additional Layer

Western nations have also aided Africa greatly through humanitarian missions. Food, clothing, education, medical care, and infrastructure have been provided to many millions of people.

GEOGRAPHY: POLITICAL MAPS OF THE U.S.

Additional Layer

Normally when we see a map of the United States depicted, the state borders are drawn in and the states colored. Draw your own map of the United States without state borders, but with major cities. Does the map look and feel different from the maps showing state borders?

What if there never were any states and America were just one single political entity? How would that have affected the history and identity of the nation? How would that affect your identity and loyalty now? Would it be better or worse?

Memorization Station

Keep working on memorizing all 50 states and capitals.

Here is a fun game to practice the states: http://deceptivelyeducational.blogspot.com/2013/01/racin-across-united-ed-states-geography.html

Maps can be used to show legal boundaries and information. These are called political maps. They don't show elevation or mountain ranges or often even rivers. But they do show you where the borders are and who lives in neighboring countries. They also show roads and cities and important places like campgrounds, national parks, and historic sites. They are maps of people, the places people live, and the things people do.

☺ ☻ EXPLORATION: Our Neighbors

Draw a map of North America freehand. Draw in the borders of the countries of North America. Include Cuba and Jamaica and other major Caribbean islands. Label each country and its capital city. Color each country a different color. Label the oceans, gulfs, and seas around North America. Color the sea blue.

Challenge older kids by having them do the map from memory. Then they can check to see how their borders ended up and whether the capitals are in the right places. Did they know the capital of Jamaica?

☺ ☻ EXPLORATION: Postal Codes

Postal codes are used when addressing a letter. It's a short way to write down which state you want your letter delivered to. Each postal code is two capital letters. For example, the postal code for Maine is ME. Maryland is MD. And Mississippi is MS.

Learn the postal codes for each state. There is a printable map at the end of this unit with postal codes written in and another blank map to quiz yourself.

☺ ☻ EXPLORATION: Road Trip

Have your kids design a road trip around America. Require that they stop in at least five different cities. Using a road map, an internet map, or the United States map from the end of this unit map your route and the distance. Figure out how long it will take to get to each destination. Do you need to stop overnight in towns? Where will you need to refuel or stop for a meal? How long will the whole trip take? What will you see along the way?

☺ ☻ EXPLORATION: Gigantic Map of the U.S.

You can print out a huge wall size map of the United States from National Geographic. http://education.nationalgeographic.com/education/maps/united-states-mapmaker-kit/?ar_a=1

The largest map is 91 sheets, but there is a 16 piece tabletop map as well. Bonus: Hawaii and Alaska get their own maps at the same scale as the rest of the United States.

You have to fit the pages together. Then just let your kids color and label to their hearts' content.

😊 🙂 EXPLORATION: Mapping Political Districts

Borders are drawn around regions or neighborhoods to mark off political districts. A political district is the area from which a candidate is elected. If you live within district 1 you get to vote for the candidate from district 1, and so on.

There are several levels of political districts. Nationally, each state functions as a district for electing its senators. Every citizen within the borders of the state can vote for two senators.

Within each state are congressional districts. The number of congressional districts in the state depends on how many people live in the state. States with high populations have more political districts than states with low populations. California has the most political districts at 53. Alaska, Montana,

This map shows the congressional districts in Missouri. Each color represents a different congressional district. A voter can only vote for the congressman who is from his district.

Delaware, North Dakota, South Dakota, Vermont, and Wyoming each have only one congressional district. The census taken every ten years is for the purpose of deciding how many representatives each state gets. So if between now and the next census there is a mass exodus from California to Montana, then California would lose congressional districts and the lines would have to be redrawn and Montana would gain congressional districts.

Read this article to learn how the lines are drawn and by whom: http://redistricting.lls.edu/who.php. You can find more specifics about your state on this site too.

You also live in a local district that elects representatives to go to your state capital and fight for the interests of your district.

Additional Layer

Gerrymandering means that political districts are drawn with odd borders to favor a particular party or candidate so they can win again and again and again. Read this article on gerrymandered districts from the 2012 elections. http://www.governing.com/blogs/by-the-numbers/most-gerrymandered-congressional-districts-states.html

This map above shows the 30th congressional district in Texas. The odd borders indicate a gerrymandered district. The lines have been drawn to ensure the winner.

Additional Layer

Another type of district is a school district or board of education. Even if you homeschool, the local school district can affect you. Who is on the school board? How are members of the school board elected and what sort of power do they have? How do they feel about homeschoolers who live in their district?

Look up information on the school district you live in. How is it organized? Do they have meetings that the public can attend?

Additional Layer

As you look at various political maps you begin to notice some patterns. For example, the larger the city is, the larger the dot on the map is that represents it. This is also true for roads. The biggest roads, especially interstates, look larger and are more clearly marked. Smaller roads, cities, and landmarks are less populated and less used, and therefore, won't be as prominent on the map.

Take a look at several maps and try to identify various things that are similar, but are differently sized between the maps.

Depending on where you live, you may also have districts that elect people for your city or county, for judges, for fire chiefs, for a sheriff, and so on. Learn about one of these types of voting districts too.

Look up information about the political districts that you live in. Where are the borders of your congressional district? Where are the borders for your local districts? Who is representing you in federal government and local government? Look in the local or state news for information or stories on your local representative. Do they work for things you agree with? Discuss this as a family.

Draw a map of either your federal congressional district or of one of your local districts. Include pictures and the names of your representatives.

☺ ☻ EXPLORATION: Population Density Maps

A population density map shows the concentration of people in certain areas. In rural areas people might be very spread out, and in cities they might be living very close together. It can be helpful to see how many people are living in particular places.

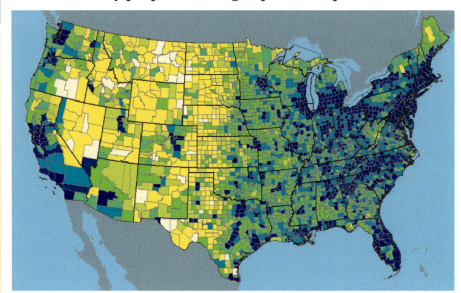

People per square mile: Dark blue: 250+; blue: 100-249; light blue: 50-99; turquoise: 25-49; green 10-24; lime green: 5-9; yellow: 1-4; white: -1

Begin with a map of the United States from the end of this unit. Using an atlas, a map from the internet, or the map above, color a population density map of the United States.

Which areas are most populated? Why do you think these areas became heavily populated? Which areas are least populated? Why are there fewer people living in these places? Do you live in an area of high population or an area of low population? How does this affect your life?

☺ EXPLORATION: City Size

Name some cities or towns you have lived in or visited. Talk about how all cities are not the same size. Some are big and some are small. List the cities you named in order of size.

Look at a map of the United States, either in an atlas or on a wall map. How do map makers show the sizes of different cities on the map? Show the kids how the symbols for the cities indicate their sizes. Find the map key and identify how the mapmakers are showing the different sizes of cities. Some maps will show population ranges while others just show relative sizes of cities. Some very small towns may not be shown at all on a map of the United States because there is not enough room. Is your city or town on the map?

Play a guessing game together. Choose a city on the map. Give clues about which city you are thinking of using cardinal directions, city size, regions, nearby cities and so on. Take turns choosing and giving clues.

☺ EXPLORATION: ZIP Codes

ZIP codes are a way for the U.S. Postal service to organize the United States into regions, cities, and postal delivery areas. ZIP stands for zone improvement plan. A postal worker can tell by looking at a zip code exactly where to send the mail without having to consult a chart or a map.

Each digit in the zip code has significance. The first digit corresponds to a region of the United States, 0-9. The next two digits refer to a large city or sectional post office. The last two digits refer to a specific post office or postal delivery area.

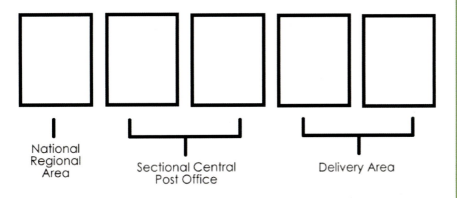

National Regional Area

Sectional Central Post Office

Delivery Area

The post office also assigns an additional 4 digit code to each address. The final four digits pinpoint the address even more specif-

Writer's Workshop

One of our favorite pre-writing activities before we write a story is to create a map of our setting. Create your own map with an imaginary kingdom, city, country, or island. Draw cities or landmarks where important events will happen in your story. You might include the characters' homes, places they adventure to, or spots where conflicts happen.

Look at some real maps to get ideas for your map. When you're finished, write your story.

On The Web

Use Google Maps to look up some interesting people-centric places on earth. Look up 10 cities and 10 other manmade landmarks.

Fabulous Fact

Political maps change faster than any other maps because our borders, country names, and other man-made things don't stay the same. Sometimes the changes are small, but sometimes they are drastic - like when the U.S.S.R. was dissolved and new countries were given independence in its place and added to the map in 1991.

ically. The first two digits in the four digit code refer to the building or street and the last two digits refer to the floor of a building or side of a street.

At the end of this unit you will find a worksheet. Color the map of the national zip code areas, and then determine the first digit for several large cities in the United States. Finally, look up and enter your zip code into the boxes on the worksheet.

☺ ☻ EXPLORATION: Map Scale

You are going to travel to seven cities in the United States: New York, Miami, Phoenix, Los Angeles, Seattle, Minneapolis, St. Louis, and then back to New York. What is the distance of the whole trip, as the crow flies?

To find the answer to this you will need a map of the United States with a scale (there is one at the end of this unit to print), a ruler, and a pencil. Measure the distance between each city with a ruler and add up the distance for the whole trip. Now consult the scale on your map and convert your ruler distance to real miles or kilometers on the ground.

On this map, below, we have drawn a line between Salt Lake City, Utah and Wichita, Kansas. We then measured the line with our ruler and compared the measurement to the scale on the map. We divided the distance from Salt Lake to Wichita by the distance on the scale and got 2.6. We then multiplied this by 300 miles (the number on the scale) and rounded the answer to 800 miles.

After you have solved our problem, have the kids set some distance problems for each other or for themselves.

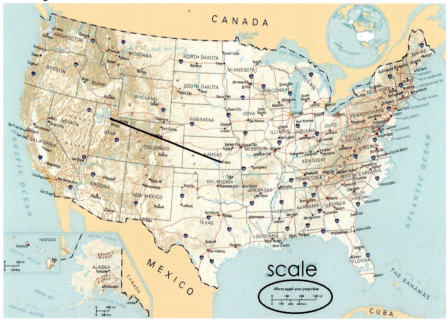

☺ ☻ EXPLORATION: City Maps

Go online and find some maps of your city. Some maps show just streets and others might include schools, parks, and tourist destinations. City maps often have a key and a scale just like state or country maps do.

Now create your own city map. It could be your city, a portion of your city, or a made up city. On your city include a key and symbols representing different locations around town. On the map below we included colors to show whether an area was residential, commercial, or industrial. We also included symbols for schools and the hospital. Parks are colored in green.

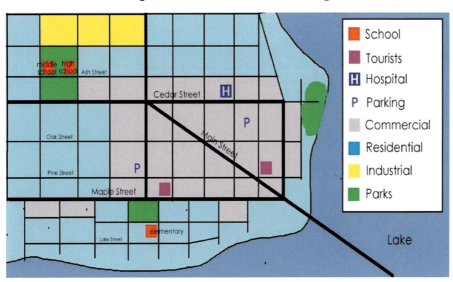

☻ ☻ EXPLORATION: Geography Pictionary

Play a game of pictionary based on U.S. geography. One child draws while the other children try to guess the word. Before you start to play you need to generate some word cards. Have the kids come up with as many geography terms and places within the United States as they can.

Ideas include: state names, major cities, mountain ranges, rivers, key, scale, zip code, road map, countries that border the United States, major bodies of water, important landmarks, and more.

You can create a game board that teams move along or just play a set number of rounds each. If you only have one or two children, have mom or dad play too, one person drawing while everyone else guesses.

Additional Layer

Use the world map printable at the end of the unit to map the locations where some of the items in your house were made. Gather fifteen or twenty items from your home. Look on the tag or on the bottom of each item to see where it was made. Put a dot on each location and label the dot with the name of the item that country produced.

Our video camera was made in Japan. Almost all of our toys were made in China. But we also had a t-shirt from Lesotho and sweat pants from Mauritius. Our toilet paper was from Canada. You might have to use an atlas to look up some of the places that aren't as familiar to you. We did!

We mapped over fifty items from our house. Most came from the United States or China. None came from Europe or South America. Are your results similar or different?

SCIENCE: ENERGY CONVERSION

Famous Folks

The Newton's Cradle is named after Isaac Newton, the famous physicist. It shows the some of the principles of motion that Newton discovered like an object in motion tends to stay in motion.

But it was actually Christiaan Huygens, a Dutch mathematician and astrologer, who used pendulums to study motion and collisions.

On the Web

This is a good video to introduce younger kids to energy conversion.

https://www.youtube.com/watch?v=ftj23FRS-2LI

This one is better for your high schoolers.

https://www.youtube.com/watch?v=fe_fFFrV-l7U

Energy conversion happens all the time - electrical energy converts to light and heat in an electrical storm, the sun's energy converts to chemical energy that is created and stored by plants, and chemical energy in food converts into motion in an animal. Potential energy converts to kinetic energy as I drop a can of tomato sauce on my toe. Whenever work is done, energy is converted.

The theory is that energy can never be lost, but only converted from one form to another. For example, if I drop a ball and let it eventually come to a rest, the potential energy that was stored in the ball while I held it in the air is converted to kinetic energy (see Unit 4-3) as it falls and then to sound energy and heat energy (friction) as it hits and slowly comes to a rest.

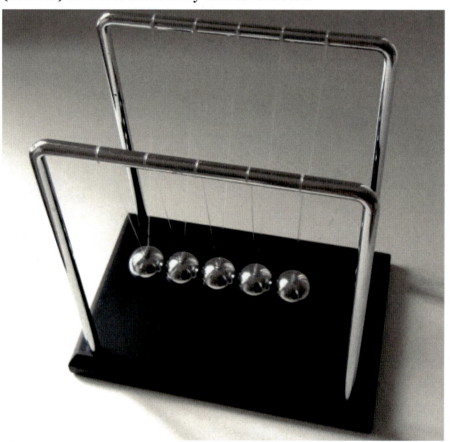

The Newton's Cradle toy, shown above, illustrates the idea of conservation of energy. If a person lifts one ball on one end and allows it to swing into the row of balls, then energy will be transferred from one ball to the next and the ball furthest on the other end of the row will swing up, then back down, transferring energy along the row again. The motion will go on unaided for awhile, but eventually it will stop. Some energy is transferred to heat, as the balls strike, and sound, as the balls make a clicking noise when hit together.

Some energy is more useful than other energy. The less useful forms we call waste energy. For example, electricity is a very useful form of energy, but for it to get to your house it must travel long distances, sometimes hundreds or thousands of miles, from the power plant where it was gathered. As it travels it has to go through wires. The wires are usually made of an aluminum alloy, which can transfer the energy along the line at high voltage. But there is some loss in the highly useful form of electric energy as some of the energy is converted into heat and some is converted into kinetic energy as the electrons collide with one another.

Think about the high quality energy used in your car, gasoline, which is converted into motion. But not all of the energy is converted into motion, is it? Where else does the energy go? The other places the energy goes is considered waste. Engineers are always trying to find ways to reduce the waste of energy whether in overhead power lines or in the engine of your car.

☻ EXPLORATION: My TV Is Powered By the Sun
Print copies of the Energy Conversion worksheet found at the end of this unit. Have your kids color the path of the energy as you talk about energy conversion.

☺ ☻ ☻ EXPERIMENT: Convert Solar Energy
Have your kids design an experiment that converts sunlight energy into heat energy that can be used for a purpose like cooking

Additional Layer

Balls have been around since ancient times. They were usually made of leather filled with air, or animals' bladders filled with air. Rubber balls were only found in the Americas.

What ball games do you like? Go outside and play a new ball game.

Additional Layer

Fireworks and firecrackers can be really fun, but they can also be dangerous. Some governments ban, regulate, or control the manufacture and sale of fireworks so that people won't hurt themselves using dangerous products.

What do you think about bans and controls on consumer goods? Should governments do that or not? Why?

food, making an environment for plants to grow better, or warming their bedroom. Make sure they write up their procedure and results and find a way of measuring their results (like by taking the temperature).

☺ ☺ ☺ EXPLORATION: Newton's Cradle

Newton's Cradle is an "executive toy" that brilliantly demonstrates some fundamental laws of physics. Play with a virtual one here: http://www.lhup.edu/~dsimanek/scenario/newton.htm.

Try lifting one ball, two balls, three balls, four balls and then all the balls at once. Before each trial predict what you think will happen. Write it down. After you try it, write down what did happen and why you think it worked the way it did.

☺ ☺ EXPERIMENT: High Flying!

You need two balls, one large and one small (like a basketball and a racket ball, a soccer ball and a tennis ball, or a big playground ball and a rubber bouncy ball).

Go outside on a concrete or asphalt surface and hold the balls so the big ball is directly below the smaller ball and the small ball rests on the big ball. Now drop both balls at the same moment.

The small ball should fly off very high. The balls hit each other just after the big ball hit the ground. The energy from the big ball was transferred to the small ball and gave it extra energy.

☺ ☺ EXPERIMENT: Firecracker

Basically, a firecracker is just gunpowder (75% potassium nitrate, 15% charcoal or sugar, and 10% sulfur) wrapped up in paper, with a fuse on it. The components of gunpowder react with each other when they are heated, so by lighting the fuse you can trigger the reaction. When you light the firecracker you are converting chemical energy into light and heat energy.

Here's a deeper look at just what happens: Lighting the firecracker with a match provides the heat source to trigger the reaction. The charcoal or sugar fuels the reaction. Potassium nitrate (KNO_3) is the oxidizer, and sulfur moderates the reaction.

C+O (from the air and the potassium nitrate) = CO_2 + energy

Potassium nitrate, sulfur, and carbon dioxide gas (the CO_2 from above) = nitrogen, carbon dioxide gas, and potassium sulfide. Pressure from the gases that are expanding explode the paper wrapper. The loud pop you hear is the paper being blown off by the high pressure from the reaction as the gases are formed.

Want to make your own? First, gather your materials:

- Scotch tape
- Black powder (you can get this from toy gun caps by opening the caps with a pin and pouring the powder out)
- Toilet paper
- Matches

Make a fuse by cutting a square of toilet paper into 6 strips. Twist one strip tightly. Use pliers to strip a match head. Put a few drops of water on the match residue to make a paste, and coat your toilet paper fuse with it. Let it dry. Cut it in half, making 2 fuses.

Take a 2 inch piece of tape and pick up the powder with the sticky side of the tape. Coat all of the stickiness with powder. Put a 2 inch long fuse on the tape about halfway down. Now roll the tape around the fuse. Use a second piece of tape to secure your powder tape around the fuse tightly. Cover the bottom of the firecracker with tape too. If you don't, your firecracker will propel like a little rocket. (You can try that next.)

Now light it! **WARNING: Make sure there's a grown-up present. Stay away from people and animals to light it. Don't hold it in your hand! Just light it, put it down, and back away.** BOOM!

😊 😊 EXPERIMENT: Energy Drink

Energy drinks contain lots of simple carbohydrates that are easy for the body to absorb and convert to mechanical energy. They also usually have salts because athletes lose a lot of salt during exercise. Most energy drinks contain a whole lot of caffeine, which is a stimulant drug, and which we don't think should ever be given to kids, so it's not in our recipe. Protein and vitamins like potassium are really important for muscle function as well. An energy drink should be a little bit sweet, but not super sweet like a soda. Too much sugar can actually make you crash; it works like a drug in your system.

So an energy drink is which type of energy conversion?

A) mechanical to electrical   C) electrical to chemical
B) chemical to mechanical   D) mechanical to electrical

Fabulous Fact

Firecrackers contain stored energy in the form of chemical energy. The stored energy is kept contained in a storage container of some kind. Traditionally it was a stalk of bamboo. Today it is usually a paper tube. When the chemical energy is ignited it explodes very quickly which blows the container up. The container blowing is what makes the fun sound.

Explanation

Many topics we cover are difficult to find in books for kids. We would like to direct you to Wikipedia.

Wikipedia is better sourced, more thorough, vastly more peer reviewed, and much more likely to have obscure topics than any other encyclopedia in the history of the world. The way they accomplish this is by the very thing Wikipedia is criticized for, namely, everyone can contribute.

Wikipedia should definitely be counted a reliable source for research and ought to be the first place everyone goes when beginning to learn about a topic.

Additional Layers

One of the reasons people drink special drinks during exercise is to replace electrolytes.

Electrolytes conduct electricity when dissolved in water. Your nervous system and muscle contractions work by moving electrical impulses across tissues. So you need electrolytes for your muscles to work properly. If you replace all of your sweat with plain water it can result in muscle cramps, lactic acid build up, and if you really overdo it, you can even die if your electrolytes get too low.

Casual exercise or playing in the backyard don't generally require electrolyte replacement, but an athlete doing two or three hour workouts does. People sick with vomiting or diarrhea also need electrolyte replacement.

On the Web

You can also use this virtual set of carts for physics experiments: http://www.physics-classroom.com/Physics-Interactives/Momentum-and-Collisions/Collision-Carts/Collision-Carts-Interactive

If you said B, then you're right on!

Here's a recipe for an energy drink that you can use to convert chemical energy (in the form of simple carbohydrates) to mechanical energy (your body moving) to win the race!

¼ cup milk
¼ tsp. salt
1 small banana
1 tsp. lemon juice
2 Tbsp. sugar

Blend it all up in a blender and enjoy. If it's hot outside, freeze your banana before you add it to make a cool smoothie.

☺ ☻ EXPLORATION: Energy Converter Quiz-o-matic

Print the Energy Conversion quiz cards you'll find at the end of this unit onto card stock. Cut apart each card. Split the kids into two teams and see who can get the most cards correct. We've marked the cards with a 1 or 2 to indicate difficulty, with 1 being the easiest and 2 the hardest. Different levels are on different pages so you can print them on different colors. The questions are hard and this material is brand new; make sure the kids know the game is a learning opportunity.

You can use the cards in conjunction with a board game like Candy Land and see who can make it to the end first. Give 5 spaces for each correct answer or something similar . . . make up your own rules.

☺ ☻ EXPERIMENT: Cart Collisions

First you need two carts, little "cars" made from blocks of wood and wheels.

You can buy carts with a study guide here: http://www.home-trainingtools.com/dynamic-carts-set-of-2/p/MC-DYNCART/

Or you can make your own. You just need two blocks of equal size and weight mounted on wheels with axles. You can use two pinewood derby kits, left raw and uncarved, just be very careful about getting the wheels in straight. My kids built two identical carts from Legos. Any of the options will satisfy the experiments.

Experiment One
Line up your two carts on a flat surface. Leave one motionless and set the other in motion, so that it crashes head-on into the first. They don't have to go fast. Observe what happens to the motion. Watch it several times and talk about what you see happening. What happens if you change the mass of one cart?

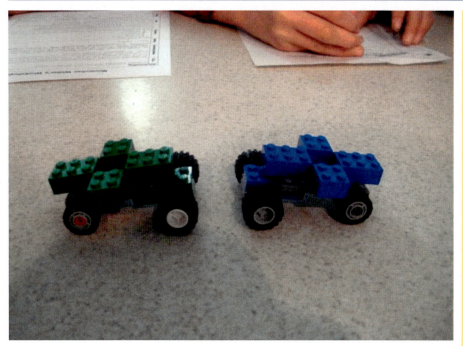

Experiment Two

Now set both of your carts in motion, at the same speed, and cause them to collide head on. What happens to their motion? What if one of the carts is much heavier than the other, now what happens when they collide? Observe the collisions several times and think about and discuss what is going on.

The Math

The cart experiments show what is happening in this equation:

$$P=mv$$

Where P equals momentum, m equals mass, and v equals velocity.

So do this calculation: You have a heavy semi-truck, but it's empty, so its mass is only 13607 kg (30,000 pounds). If it's going 27 meters per second (60 miles per hour), what is its momentum?

Now the trucker loads the truck with milk cartons and the load's mass increases to 31751 kg (70,000 pounds). What is the momentum now of the truck and load at 27 meters per second?

You have a beautiful Honda Civic with a mass of 1133 kg (2,500 pounds). It too is traveling at 27 meters per second. What is the momentum of the Honda Civic?

Explanation

In our cart experiments we were causing the carts to collide and the energy was transferred from one cart to the other. What hap-

Teaching Tip

In the collision problems the equation uses mass, but we are actually using the weight. How are mass and weight related? The mass of an object is fixed, but weight depends on gravitational pull.

As long as the two systems you are comparing (the truck and the car) are in the same gravitational pull, the calculations comparing them will work out. But if we moved our Honda to the moon, we'd have to convert to mass by dividing each number by the gravity of their location.

Fabulous Fact

When scientists use words sometimes they mean something different than you would mean. The word collision, scientifically, means any time two bodies with mass touch for a short time. It does not have to be a violent interaction. For example, a collision occurs when a bee lands briefly on a flower.

Scientists use very precise language so they can understand one another clearly. What if the rest of us were that precise with language?

Additional Layer

Momentum is the combination of speed and mass. So if two vehicles are moving at the same speed but one is twice as heavy as the other, then the momentum of the heavier one is greater.

A video on momentum: https://www.youtube.com/watch?v=uQ1UM-HXyFrM

On the Web

Here is a slow motion video of a car crash: https://www.youtube.com/watch?v=BZQMfb-5naz8

pened if one of the carts weighed more than the other? What would happen to the momentum of the truck and car if they were to collide head on? Where would the momentum and energy go?

Remember that energy in a closed system is conserved, so in our cart experiments we saw that the amount of momentum in the cart in motion was exactly transferred to the other cart upon collision. If both carts were in motion and they both weighed exactly the same amount and were going the same speed, then when they collided head on they should both bounce back with the same momentum they hit with. If one cart weighed more, then the lighter cart would bounce back more than the heavier one.

In our calculations of the milk delivery truck and the Honda Civic we see that the momentum of the truck is much greater than the momentum of the little car, even though they are going the same speed. If they collide head on at 27 meters per second (60 mph), what do you think the motion of the two bodies would look like?

☻ EXPERIMENT: Elastic Collisions

An elastic collision is one in which no momentum is lost, no damage occurs, and no heat is produced. Remember our Newton's cradle? It is an elastic collision, or would be in a vacuum where no energy could be lost to sound and very little to friction. The balls would keep bouncing forever. When a pool ball is struck by another, the first ball stops and the second acquires all the momentum of the first ball; momentum is conserved. It is an elastic collision.

Here is the equation:

$$m_1 u_1 + m_2 u_2 = m_1 v_1 + m_2 v_2$$

u stands for speed before the collision, v stands for speed after the collision, and m is for mass. The 1's and the 2's tell you which object you are dealing with, object 1 or object 2.

For a collision we can also write another equation:

$$K + Q = K$$

In this equation K stands for kinetic energy and Q stands for the amount of kinetic energy either gained or lost in the collision. An elastic collision is defined as Q being 0, energy is neither gained nor lost.

If kinetic energy is lost in the collision, then Q will be less than 0 and if kinetic energy is gained then Q will be more than 0.

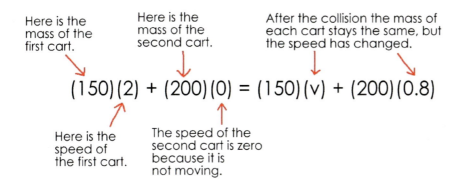

Situations where kinetic energy is lost are called inelastic collisions (see next exploration). If kinetic energy is gained, then there must be something like a spring, or an explosion, potential, or chemical energy stored somewhere in the system. This sort of collision is called a super-elastic collision.

The only truly elastic collisions have to take place where the two objects don't actually touch, like atoms of a gas bouncing around in a closed system. They repel one another and don't ever touch, and don't lose any energy to noise, heat, or other forms of kinetic energy. Whatever energy is in the system will remain in the system unless external factors interfere. The carts and billiard balls actually lose some of their kinetic energy to friction and sound.

So try it out. Let's say that two carts (we'll assume they are in a perfect system and lose none of their energy to sound or friction) are about to collide. The first cart weighs 150 grams and is traveling at 2 meters per second. The second cart weighs 200 grams and is not moving. After the collision the second cart is traveling at 0.8 meters per second. How fast is the first cart moving?

Memorization Station

The first law of thermodynamics says that energy can be transformed (or converted) but it cannot be destroyed.

Additional Layer

Perpetual motion machines can do work indefinitely without an energy source. Of course, this is impossible because of the first law of thermodynamics (see above) and the second law of thermodynamics, which states that entropy always increases. Therefore useful energy will always degrade into less useful energy. In the process of motion, bodies are always subject to friction, heat, or dissipation of energy in some other way. Even the motion of the planets around the sun will not continue forever.

Perpetual motion machines and the quest to make them is much like the alchemical quest to turn lead into gold or the chemical search for the universal solvent.

So as not to sound quacky, modern designers of the elusive perpetual motion machine called them "overunity" instead.

Additional Layer

Take a tour of your home and find machines, devices, or processes where energy is being converted from one form to another.

Identify which types of energy are involved.

Here are some examples of things you might have in your home:

- Microphone
- Fireplace
- Car engine
- Electric heater
- Refrigerator
- Food
- Generator
- Battery

On the Web

This excellent video explains elastic and inelastic collisions.

https://www.youtube.com/watch?v=Xe2r-6wey26E&nohtml5=-False

Fabulous Fact

All energy that humans use on earth comes from either the sun or from the earth in the form of thermal, chemical, or nuclear energy. Energy is a finite resource, but as long as the sun shines and the earth remains thermodynamically active we will have energy.

Set up your equation by replacing the letters with the values you already know:

$$(150)(2) + 200(0) = (150)v + (200)(0.8)$$

Now we solve for the after collision velocity of the first cart algebraically. First I'll multiply each of the terms:

$$300 + 0 = 150v + 160$$

Now subtract the 160 from both sides:

$$140 = 150v$$

Finally we can divide the 150 from both sides:

$$.933 = v$$

You can check your answer by calculating the total kinetic energy for before and after the collision.

$$(150)(2) + (200)(0) = (150)(.933) + (200)(0.8)$$

If you cut a little slack for rounding errors, the two sides come out equal.

In the equation above we started with one object not moving, velocity zero. But if both objects are moving before collision then one direction of movement needs to be assigned a negative number and the other direction a positive number for the velocity. This does not mean that one object is moving at less than zero velocity; the negatives and positives just stand for directions and make your equation come out properly.

You can try more equations with the worksheet in the printables section at the end of this unit.

☻ EXPLORATION: Inelastic Collisions

A collision is inelastic if part of the kinetic energy is converted into other forms. If your car crumples in a crash then some (hopefully a whole lot) of the kinetic energy is absorbed by the crumpling metal and the friction of the road and the wrenching sound of tearing metal. This is an inelastic collision.

Let's envision the perfect inelastic collision and do an equation for it.

You are very carefully standing still in the middle of an extremely slippery patch of ice. Your friend, who weighs exactly the same amount as you (50 kg), comes sliding across the ice toward you at 1 meter per second. You collide, he wraps his arms around you, and you are now both traveling together in the same direction at exactly half the speed your friend was traveling at to begin with.

In a perfectly inelastic collision the two objects are stuck together and become one in terms of motion and mass. Most collisions in the real world are inelastic, but not perfectly inelastic.

Here is the equation:

$$m_1 v_1 + m_2 v_2 = (m_1 + m_2) v_2$$

$$(50)(1) + (50)(0) = (50 + 50)(v)$$
$$50 = 100v$$
$$.5 \text{ mps} = v$$

Think up some inelastic collision scenarios and write a few problems. Exchange with a friend and solve.

☺ ☺ ☺ EXPLORATION: Rube-Goldberg Machine

Use the energy concepts you've learned to create your own Rube-Goldberg machine. A Rube-Goldberg machine is a silly, complicated contraption that performs a simple task. You'll need to gather supplies like dominoes, marbles, bouncy balls, cardboard tubes, blocks, pvc pipe, string, bottles, foil, and other materials you want to incorporate into your machine. Decide on a task you would like your machine to perform. Look up a few Rube-Goldeberg machines on the internet to watch in action for inspiration. Then build your machine.

Self-Operating Napkin

Famous Folks

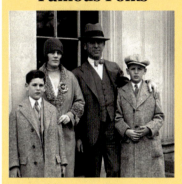

Reuben Goldberg was born in 1883 in California. He loved drawing cartoons, but his dad wanted him to be an engineer, not a comic artist. He was unhappy in that job though, and went back to his passion - drawing cartoons in newspapers.

He made a crazy chain reaction series of cartoons with complicated contraptions that performed simple tasks. They become really popular, and cartoonists and inventors alike are still creating Rube-Goldberg machines inspired by his cartoons.

ARTS: IMPRESSIONISM I

Explanation

We'll be covering Impressionist art during Units 4-5 and 4-6. Unit 4-5 will discuss the entire movement and the kinds of new techniques and ideas that painters from this school utilized. Then in Unit 4-6 we'll learn about famous Impressionist artists and their art.

Teaching Tip

Discuss the elements of art (line, shape, texture, color, and space) during this unit as you look at Impressionist paintings. Compare the elements of a famous painting from another era with these. How do they differ? For example, the lines are soft, blurred, and indiscreet on Impressionist paintings when compared with Rococo art. What other differences do you notice?

Fabulous Fact

Impressionism is considered the first modern art movement.

The Impressionists broke from tradition and ushered in a new beginning in the world of art.

The art movement called Impressionism began in the 1860s and lasted through the 1870s and 1880s. Impressionist painters were not popular. They were thought to be rebellious frauds in the art world, chucking out the conventions and rules that artists had developed and followed for centuries.

The real ruckus began when the Impressionists defied the elite official Salon in Paris. For hundreds of years, anyone who was anyone in the art world wanted to have their work displayed at the annual Salon. Each year select artists were invited to show pieces in the special exhibition. It was an amazing honor to be selected and meant fame for the artists. But over and over again the Impressionists were highly criticized and denied by the panel who selected pieces for the Salon. The critics said their style was too different; they were just trying to be controversial; their pieces looked unfinished. Having had enough, the young painters decided to make their own exhibition.

In 1874 Monet, Renoir, Pissarro, Sisley, Degas, Cezanne, and Berthe Morisot set up their own exhibition, determined to show the public the paintings they had been creating over the past decade. This small group of artists continued on, holding eight exhibitions in all, painting together, and sharing ideas about new ways to paint and see nature and the world around them.

The small group of painters liked to capture moments in time. They quickly painted the moments, not taking as much care with careful planning and detail as their predecessors had. They used larger, more casual brush strokes. They painted straight on the canvas without doing sketches and studies beforehand. They filled the canvas with bright colors, loved to explore light, and had little care for perfect technique.

😊 😊 😊 EXPLORATION: Impressionism 101

For much of the history of art there was one important goal held by artists: make the painting look real. Most of the advances of art dealt with techniques of making the subjects of paintings look real, from the perfect colors, shading, and proportion to the tiniest details and symbolisms. Perfect technique was the goal.

Impressionist painters threw out that entire idea, wanting instead to capture light and communicate an experience. Realism was replaced by "impressions." The idea was to capture a moment, not clearly defined or studied, just experienced.

For this exploration, let's look at two paintings, one Impressionist painting and one that was done over 200 years before. Both are by famous painters. Both are cityscapes that feature the sea in the foreground. Both show European port cities.

The View of Delft by Johannes Vermeer was a Baroque painting from the 1660s. It looks almost like a postcard. Try as you might, you won't see individual brush strokes on its surface. The coloration and shading look almost perfect. The shadows cast by the

Additional Layer

These events were also happening in the world while the Impressionists painted:

- American Civil War
- Austro-Prussian War
- Swedish chemist Alfred Nobel invented dynamite
- First telephone conversation by Alexander Graham Bell
- Franco-Prussian War
- Blue jeans were patented by Levi Strauss and Jacob Davis
- Huge volcano at Krakatoa erupted
- Invention of the phonograph by Thomas Edison
- Creation of the Statue of Liberty
- The Emancipation Proclamation freeing U.S. Slaves
- First Kentucky Derby
- First cash register was invented
- American Red Cross established by Clara Barton
- The Orient Express began running between Paris and Constantinople
- Eiffel Tower constructed

Fabulous Fact

These are some hallmarks of Impressionism that you can look for when you see art from this era:

- Using color, and especially blending colorful brush strokes to create interesting textures

- Natural light that is less dramatic than the heavy light and shade of earlier paintings

- Outdoor scenes, partly because artists were actually taking their paints and canvases outside to paint rather than working inside studios

- Paintings of Paris and its surrounding countyside and seashore

- Blurred scenes that tried to show the very impressions of a moment in time rather than details

- Less concern with realism

- Less focus on religious and historical paintings.

On The Web

A good introductory look at Impressionism:

https://youtu.be/kuOo-nogw-TM

buildings are realistic. The details on the buildings and ships are precise, tiny, and intricate. The whole painting feels balanced, unified, and a perfect mix of light and shade. Vermeer even mixed very fine sand in with some of the paint on the window frames of the buildings to give them a textured quality.

Now, let's fast forward 200 years or so to this painting of a harbor by Claude Monet called *Port of Le Havre*.

We still see the water, the buildings, and the boats, but this Impressionist painting looks completely different. Not at all like a postcard, it looks almost blurry by comparison. It doesn't take more than a glance to see the large, visible brush strokes. The colors are softer and seem to run together. The shadows are present, but inconsistent and not well defined. The whole thing seems lighter, without a distinct difference between light and shade.

Art critics hated this new style. In fact, they didn't see it as anything more than sloppy, shoddy work, not worth a place in the art world. But Monet and the other Impressionists were on to something. Their quickly done paintings of moments and impressions sparked a whole new wave of art that led to lots of other artistic experiments. This was the begin of a new era - modern art.

And strangely enough, even with the perfection of Vermeer's harbor, I would rather have the Monet hanging on my wall.

Write about each of the paintings and the differences you observe between them. What qualities do you see in Monet's painting that you can look for in other Impressionist paintings? What makes a great painting? Which one would you rather have on your wall and why?

EXPLANATION: Impression Sunrise

Impressionism was given its name by an art critic who published an article about the 1874 exhibition. He was not a fan of the style, and his piece was not complimentary, but the name stuck. He used a painting called *Impression Sunrise* by Claude Monet as an example of the style, which most people felt looked sloppy and unfinished. The painting was actually of the same harbor, the Port of Le Havre, that we looked at in the previous exploration, but this version of it was even less defined.

☺ ☺ ☺ EXPLORATION: En Plein Air

The Impressionists painted en plein air, or outside. They did not sit in studios. They went to the scene they were painting and captured that moment. Partly this trend was made possible because for the first time, painters in the 1800s could easily buy tubes of paint rather than grinding their own pigments. Paint became portable, and many painters moved outside to do their work.

Go outside to make your own picture "en plein air." First, make a viewfinder by cutting some card stock into a simple frame. Take your viewfinder outside and use it to "frame in" the picture you want to paint or draw in your sketchbook. Hold it up in front of your chosen scene and imagine it as your finished piece.

A trick that artists use, especially when they are outside working and don't have a lot of tools with them, is to use their thumbs to help them make items in their picture that are to scale.

Fabulous Fact

Impressionist painters painted quickly. They wanted to capture a scene before the light changed, so they had to work fast. One of the reasons you see lots of dabs of color is because it was faster to brush on the colors you intended to mix than to actually perfectly mix each one on the palette. They let our eyes do the job of color mixing.

Additional Layer

Charles Francois Daubigny took the idea of painting outside to a whole new level. He bought a 28 foot ferry boat and made it into a floating studio with living quarters, inspiring Monet to do the same. Learn more about Daubigny.

Famous Folks

Gustave Courbet was not an Impressionist painter, but his ideas sparked a new idea that Impressionists adopted. Courbet was a Realist. At first that may seem like the very opposite of Impressionism, but he did something they liked. He painted people and things as they really are, not with perfect symmetry and no flaws. Even though Impressionists didn't mimic his style, they did mimic his idea that they should paint an honest version of things.

Additional Layer

If you make four versions of your painting from the *Everything Changes, Even Stone* Exploration, you can cut them each into fourths and glue one fourth of each in place to show one scene in four different lights.

This person is about two thumbs tall and the mountain behind is about four thumbs tall at its peak. It's not a careful measurement, but when you're outside and don't have a studio full of measuring and sketching tools, it will do. Choose a scene through your viewfinder and then use your thumb to approximate sizes as you paint an outdoor scene.

😊 😊 😊 **EXPLORATION: Impressionist Painting Lesson**
Gather these supplies:

- Acrylic paints in white, yellow, orange, deep red, green, cobalt blue, navy blue, and deep violet.
- A canvas
- Brushes
- Water

Now go watch "How to paint like Monet: Lessons on Impressionist landscape painting techniques - Part 1" (https://youtu.be/xI-Cl4l3P57k), a YouTube video that demonstrates how to create an Impressionist style painting in a series of several episodes.

😊 😊 **EXPLORATION: Everything Changes, Even Stone**
Claude Monet once wrote in a letter, "Everything changes. Even stone."

As were many of the Impressionists, he was fascinated by light and how it changed the whole scene he was painting. He often painted many versions of the very same scene, but cast in different lights at different times of the day.

These are all paintings he made of the Rouen Cathedral.

Paint a scene in your sketchbook at three different times of day - one in the morning, one in the afternoon, and one in the evening near the time of sunset. Paint quickly to try to capture the moment before the light changes, and use a color palette that reflects the lighting at the moment, not just the color of the item as you see it in your mind. For example, at sunset a red barn may actually look dark blue or almost black if there isn't much light.

😊 😊 😊 EXPLORATION: Vibrant Color

If you did the Impressionist Painting Lesson video you saw that one of the techniques was putting a colorful undercoat below our initial painting. Color was important to Impressionist painters. They didn't just add black to a hue to make a color darker nor just add white to make it lighter. They were interested in the subtle differences that light had on a scene and tried to imitate them by mixing many colors together. You can have fun with color mixing in a new way in this exploration. Use acrylic paints on a paper plate to mix colors. When you grab paint with your brush start with a tiny amount so you'll be able to make many adjustments without using up too much paint. Be especially careful as you add dark colors. It can be difficult to lighten a color that has gotten too dark. Here are a few interesting color experiments to try:

- Add blue to orange to make a rich, dark orange color
- Add purple to yellow to make a dark yellow.
- Mix orange and green together to make light brown.

Additional Layer

Monet painted lots of versions of the same thing, but with different lighting and coloration.

We implement this same technique digitally now. Professional and amateur photographers alike use photo filters to change the light, color, texture, tone, and contrast to their photos. Photo editing software right down to simple apps can change the appearance of photos in no time.

Be a modern day Monet. Try your hand at photo filters and see if you can transform the way a photo looks.

Additional Layer

Try the *Everything Changes, Even Stone Exploration* using a different medium: photography. We can now capture a moment (an impression) in an instant with photography. Use your camera to capture the same scene in the morning, in the afternoon, and near sunset. You might even extend this across days, capturing sunny versus cloudy days, cold versus hot, and so on. Does everything change as Monet thought?

Explanation

When I visit art galleries that have Impressionist paintings I find it interesting to look at each painting from close up and from far away. From very close it can be difficult to tell what the picture is sometimes; instead, you just notice the brush strokes and paint.

When you stand back several feet (8 to 12 feet) and take a look at the whole thing all at once, it looks very different. You begin to see the entire scene and the brush strokes fade away.

Can you see the spot on this painting where the close up image above came from?

- Mix green and purple together to make dark brown.
- Try to make gray tones without using black and white. Can you find a combination that makes gray?
- Use dark blue instead of black to create shadows.

Try using the colors you created to paint a scene that is completely colorful, with no black or white paint anywhere.

☺ ☺ ☺ **EXPLORATION: Dots, Dashes, and Stipples**

Visible brush strokes were the main point of criticism when it came to Impressionist paintings. Art critics hated how they could see every brush stroke on the paintings. Impressionists didn't mind the visible brush strokes though.

Begin by painting a simple picture of a goldfish on a blue background. Let your goldfish dry completely before you continue.

Practice making a variety of visible brush strokes. When you don't mind if your brush strokes show you can use larger, stiffer paintbrushes. Your paint can also be rather dry, so don't get your paintbrush wet before you start.

First, paint in small dots. Add dots to the main body of your fish using different colors. You might try white, cream, yellow, orange, red, brown, or combinations of these. Use a stiff round brush. When you stand back and look at the painting later your eye will blend the dots into a color, but when you look up close you will see the many colors of individual dots.

Second, paint in dashes. For dashes you will need a stiff, flat brush. You can lightly press and lift for smaller dashes, or you can use a dry flat brush to make short sweeps for dashes that are a bit bigger and more pronounced. Add dashes to the fins and tail. You can either just choose one color of dashes or several.

Third, paint stipples. Stippling is putting many very tiny dots on top of other layers of paint. If you want the stippled colors to run together, use a wet brush and several colors over the top of each other. If you want the stipples to be more distinct, use a dry brush and let individual colors dry before adding more. Add stipples to the water around your fish.

😊 😊 EXPLORATION: Light and Shadow

Shine a light on an object you'd like to paint. You can use a desk lamp and a small object like an apple, a houseplant, or a simple shaped toy. Situate your light so it is off to one side. This will create one area that is well lit and one area that has a strong shad-

ow on it. Now use watercolor paints in your sketchbook or on thick watercolor paper to experiment with painting the object. Instead of just adding black or gray to create the shadowy side, use the color of the object and then add a bit of blue into the color you painted your object to make it get gradually darker.

Look at the shadows in this painting by Monet and compare it with the shadows in your painting. He used lots of different colors to make the haystacks and the shadows they are creating.

😊 😊 😊 EXPLORATION: Paris

Napoleon III, the last monarch of France, ordered that Paris be remodeled beginning in the 1850s. The streets were widened, beautiful public parks and fountains were created, public toilets

On The Web

A demonstration of Impressionist brush-strokes and color mixing: https://youtu.be/RsD-pE1UJv7w

Fabulous Fact

Impressionism may not have been popular in its day, but we have since come to admire it much more. This famous painting by Renoir once sold for over $78 million.

Additional Layer

Colorful shadows were captured in this painting by Mary Cassatt. In the portrait, Lydia is waiting for an opera to begin. Can you spot the different shades between the shadows on her dress and on her chair?

Famous Folks

Baron Georges-Eugene Haussmann was the city planner who designed the new Paris under Napoleon III. He planned and oversaw the Paris project for many years until, when it was almost finished, he was dismissed from his post after harsh criticism, mostly due to people growing tired of the expensive and intrusive construction project. Though somewhat unpopular in his day, he is now given credit for modernizing and beautifying the city of Paris. He tore down much of the city in the process, but his vision was realized and Paris was rebuilt far better than it had ever been before. We still use the term "Haussmannization" to mean the creative destruction of a thing for the betterment of society.

were added, new aqueducts and a sewer system were installed under the city, and over 40,000 new buildings were built. The city was transformed.

Painters became inspired by the transformation and the bustling new city they saw before them. Along with outdoor landscapes, cityscapes became popular among Impressionist painters.

If you look at Impressionist art you are bound to see glimpses of Paris. It was the meeting place of this rebellious group of painters, and their city had been transformed before their very eyes.

Make your own cityscape of Paris. You can be as imaginative and unrealistic as you like. Use lots of color and create whatever your impression of the city is rather than making a realistic view.

Gustave Caillebotte painted this interesting cityscape of Paris in 1875. You can see the newly remodeled city through the window his brother is looking through.

This one was made by drawing the Eiffel Tower in the foreground surrounded by bushes. A landscape line sits above, housing the colorful buildings of Paris. It was sketched with permanent markers and then filled in with colorful patterns using colored pencils.

The Eiffel Tower was actually added to Paris a few years after the city remodel, in preparation for the World's Fair in 1889. Today you can hardly make a Paris cityscape without this iconic tower though.

☺ ☺ ☺ **EXPLORATION: Mini Impressionist Gallery**

The Impressionists were not at all tied down to their studios. They painted things they saw all around them. Portable tubes of paint made it easy to paint en plein air. City renovations inspired them to paint their new surroundings. Better trains and public transportation meant that a trip to the surrounding countryside or to the seashore on the coast was a simple journey. Nature and light inspired them. Before you make your own gallery, look at many Impressionist paintings in a gallery, an art book, or on the internet. Get a feel for their style and point out similarities you notice between the paintings.

Create your own miniature Impressionist gallery in your sketchbook. Begin with the gallery printable from the printables section.

In each frame create your own small work of art based on the art of the Impressionists. Create your impressions of each of the scenes, and don't worry about being realistic. Use the brush strokes you've practiced during this unit and be creative with colors and light. You'll be creating a Paris scene, a countryside vista, a seascape, and a picture of the sky. Think about how the Impressionists would have portrayed each of these scenes and paint in their style.

Fabulous Fact

Georges Seurat was inspired by the original group of Impressionist painters and made a lot of paintings in their style. He made a beautiful Impressionist cityscape of the Eiffel Tower in 1889, the year of the World's Fair in Paris. He was famous for using colorful dots to create his paintings in a style called Pointillism.

Coming up next . . .

Unit 4-6

The West
Southwest States
Earth Structure
Impressionism II

My ideas for this unit:

Title: _____ **Topic:** _____

_____
_____
_____
_____
_____
_____
_____
_____
_____
_____

Title: _____ **Topic:** _____

_____
_____
_____
_____
_____
_____
_____
_____
_____
_____

Title: _____ **Topic:** _____

_____
_____
_____
_____
_____
_____
_____
_____
_____
_____

Title: _____ **Topic:** _____

_____

_____

_____

_____

_____

_____

_____

_____

_____

_____

Title: _____ **Topic:** _____

_____

_____

_____

_____

_____

_____

_____

_____

_____

_____

_____

Title: _____ **Topic:** _____

_____

_____

_____

_____

_____

_____

_____

_____

_____

_____

Colonization of Africa

Throughout its history Africa was made up of many different tribes, peoples, and civilizations, each with their own history and heritage. In the 1800's many European countries claimed the lands of Africa as their own. Taking ownership of and colonizing the area.

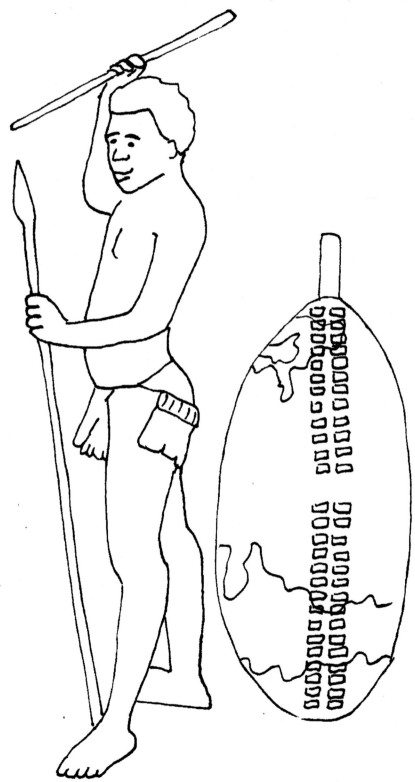

African Colonialism: Unit 4-5 Timeline

1652 **4-5** Dutch colonize the Cape of Good Hope as a weigh station for ships sailing to India 	**1806** **4-5** England takes Cape colony from Dutch, as part of Napoleonic wars 	**1816** **4-5** Shaka becomes king of the Zulus and systematically conquers all his neighbors, depopulating southern Africa in the process 	**1836-1845** **4-5** Great Trek 
1838 **4-5** Boers defeat the Zulus in battle 	**1841** **4-5** David Livingstone begins to explore Africa 	**1879** **4-5** Zulus are defeated by British 	**1880** **4-5** French make a treaty turning the land north of the Congo into a French protectorate. 
1881 **4-5** Tunisia becomes a French protectorate 	**1882** **4-5** British take sole rule of Egypt when the French pull out 	**1882** **4-5** Italy takes control of Eritrea 	**1884** **4-5** European nations make treaties dividing Africa 

1885 4-5	1896 4-5	1902 4-5	1904-05 4-5
Congo Free State established by Leopold II	Italy defeated by Ethiopia at the Battle of Adwa	British defeat the Boers in South Africa	Herero of Namibia rise up against German overlords
1905 4-5	1912 4-5		
Maji-Maji rebel against German rule in East Africa	Zulus unite to become the South African National Congress, which becomes the African National Congress (ANC)		

Covered Wagons of the Trekkers

South Africa 1900

Scramble for Africa

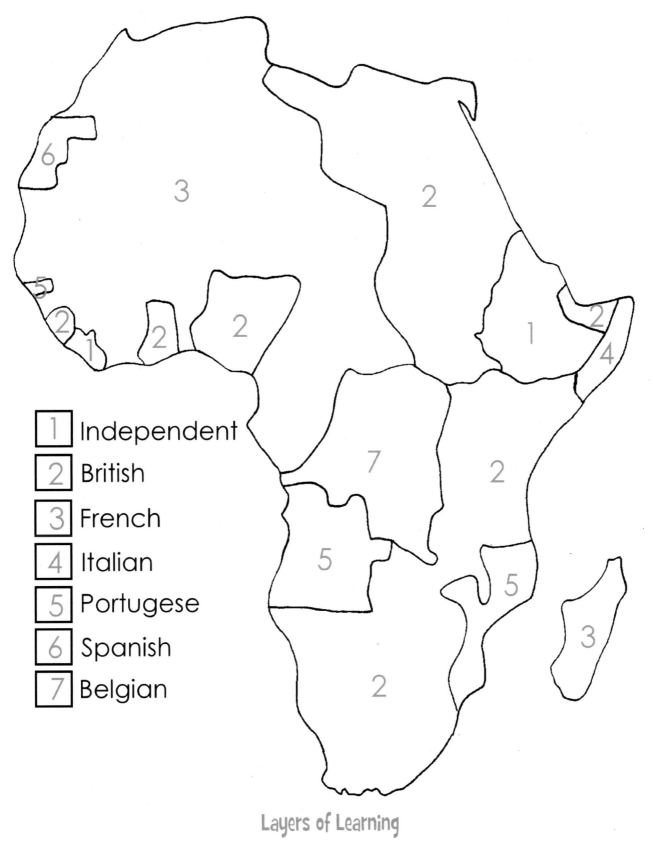

1 Independent
2 British
3 French
4 Italian
5 Portugese
6 Spanish
7 Belgian

Postal Codes of the United States

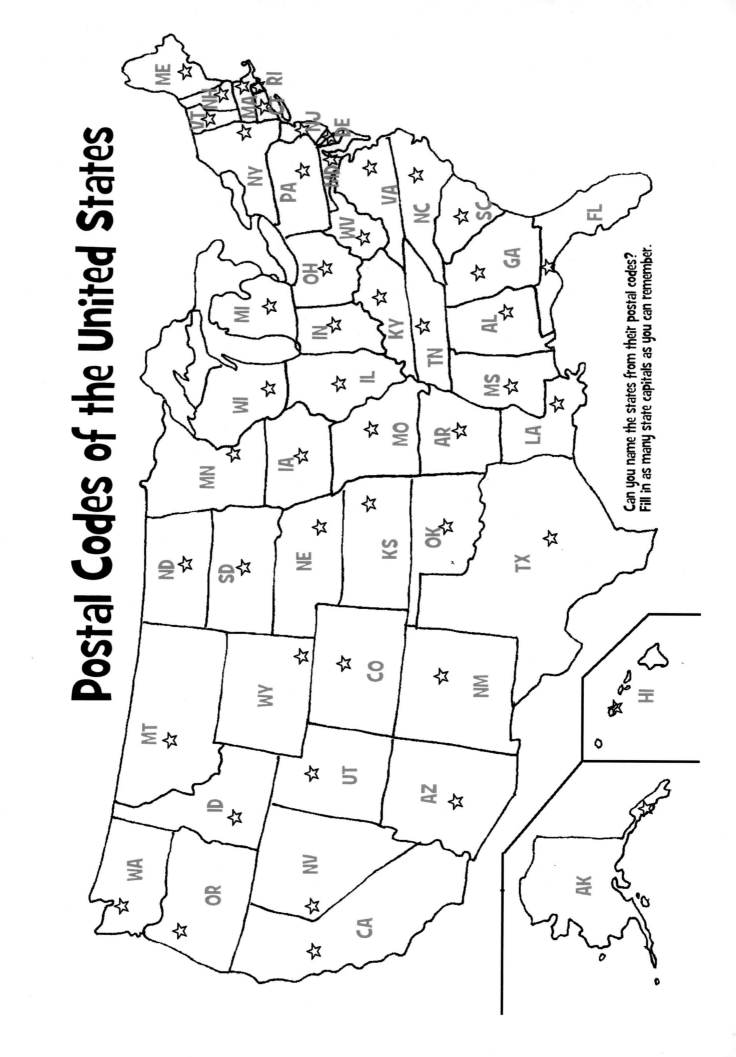

Can you name the states from their postal codes?
Fill in as many state capitals as you can remember.

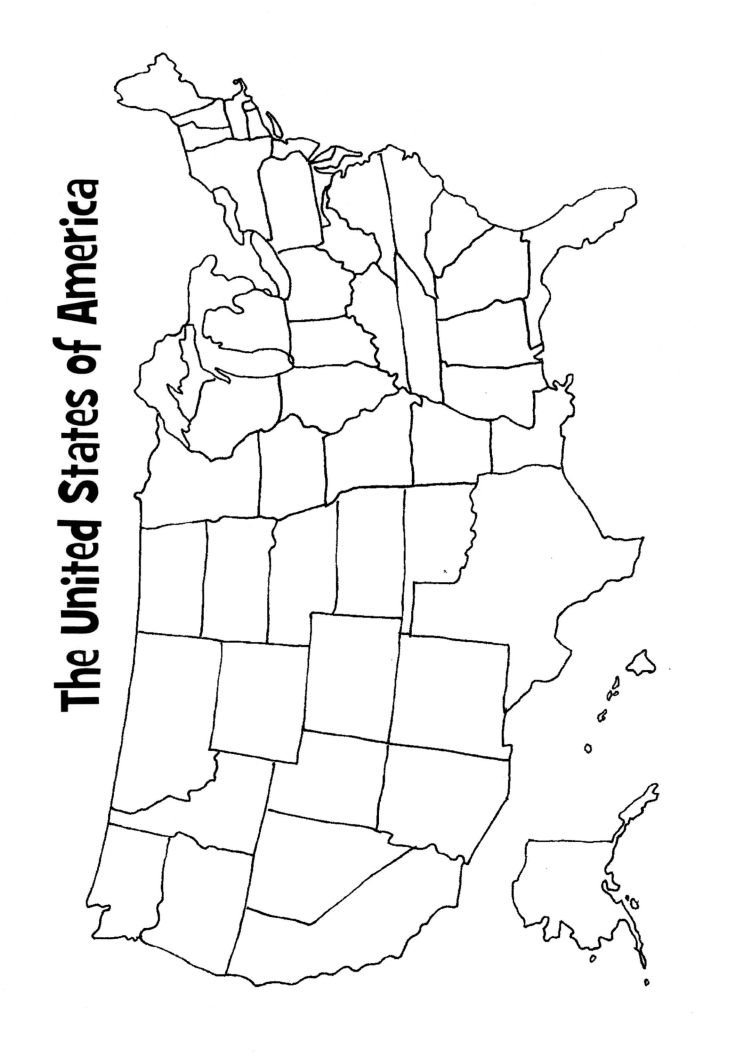

The United States of America

United States Zip Codes

Color each zip code a different color in the map below.

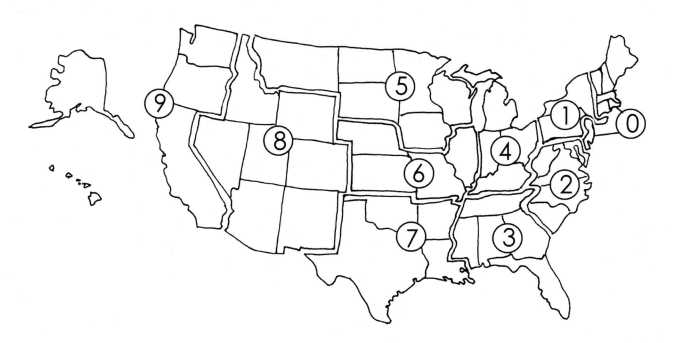

Find the first digit of the zip code for each of these cities. You may need a map of the United States to determine in which state each city is located.

San Francisco _____   Arlington _____   Detroit _____

Dallas _____   Cleveland _____   Boston _____

Salt Lake City _____   Honolulu _____   Atlanta _____

Kansas City _____   Denver _____   Providence _____

Write down your zip + 4 in the boxes below. If you don't know it, you can find it by typing your address into a search engine with the words "zip code".

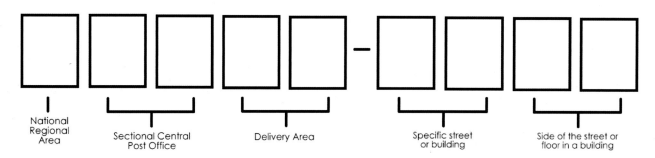

National Regional Area

Sectional Central Post Office

Delivery Area

Specific street or building

Side of the street or floor in a building

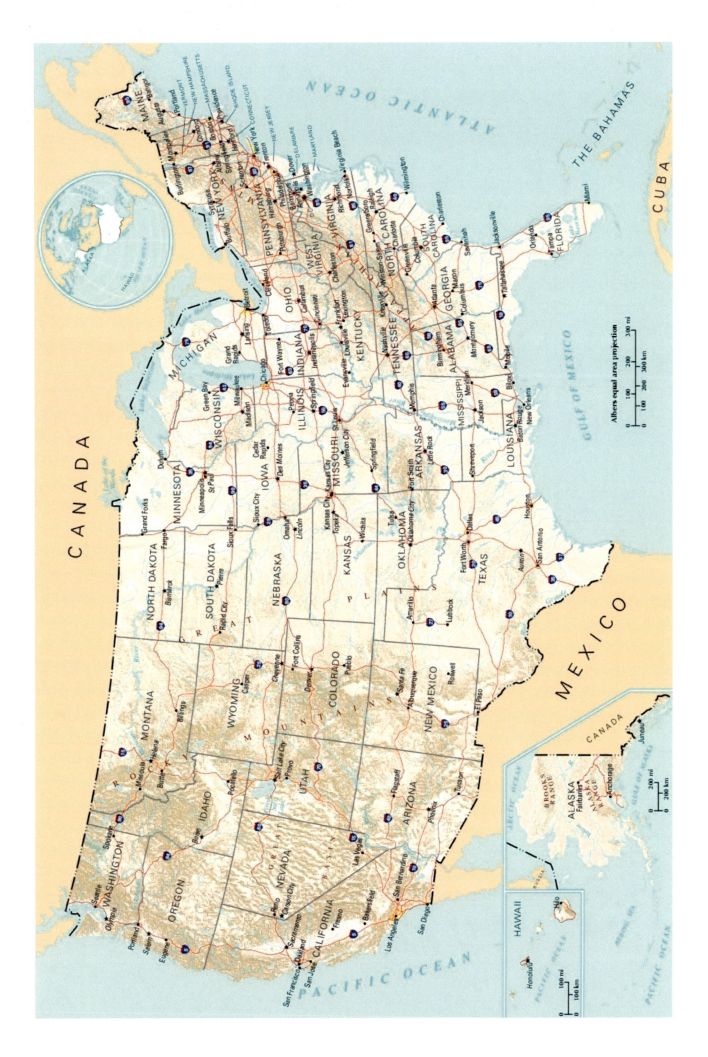

Energy Conversion

Sunlight energy is converted into . . .

heat energy, which evaporates water . . . .

and causes clouds to form, which are blown into the mountains, where the water gathers . . . .

and forms powerful rivers that turn turbines in a dam . . . .

which changes the kinetic energy of the river into electrical energy . . . .

which powers my television.

Energy Conversion Quiz-o-matic

1 Energy from food is which kind of energy? Mechanical or chemical Chemical	1 T or F Energy is never lost, it is just converted from one form to another. T

1 T or F Energy is needed to do work. T	1 Sunlight is which type of energy? Chemical or electromagnetic Electromagnetic	1 T or F Energy conversion is a long complicated math problem. F
1 If energy is never lost why doesn't a ball keep bouncing forever? a) it converts energy to friction and sound b) it does bounce forever a	1 Which type of energy is sound? Electromagnetic or mechanical? Mechanical	1 T or F Kinetic and potential energy are both energy of motion. F, kinetic is energy of motion, but potential energy is stored.
1 Which of these energy types is most useful? a) gasoline in your car's tank b) heat coming off your car's engine a	1 Which of these types of energy is the chemical energy in a firework not converted into. a) light b) electrical b	1 T or F Kinetic energy is really just another way of saying the energy of motion. T

2 As a ball falls to the ground its potential energy is converted into which type of energy? Kinetic	2 What is another name for light energy? Electromagnetic	2 T or F Every time energy is converted to a new form some is converted into non-useful forms. T
2 A compressed spring has which type of energy? Potential	2 What is energy conversion? Energy being changed from one form to another.	2 What is the law of conservation of energy? It says that energy can neither be created nor destroyed, only changed in form.
2 The sun is powered by nuclear energy. This is: a) chemical energy b) electromagnetic energy c) potential energy d) kinetic and thermal d	2 Which type of energy is sugar? Chemical energy	2 Where in the body is chemical energy stored? Fat and muscle both are chemical energy storage.
2 What type of energy is sound? Mechanical, sound is produced by waves in the air.	2 Name one useful and one not-very-useful type of energy. Answers vary. The motion of a train and heat coming out a train smokestack would be one example.	2 Electrical energy is converted into which type of energy when you recharge batteries? Chemical

Elastic Equations Practice Problems

Assume that there is no friction and that the kinetic energy is conserved.

Thomas set two air hockey pucks on the air hockey table, each weighing 50 grams. He sent one flying across the table at 25 meters per second to the left and the other at 10 meters per second to the right so that they collided with one another and bounced straight back. After the collision, the second puck was traveling at 18 meters per second to the left. How fast was the second puck traveling?

Two star ships were drifting aimlessly toward one another. The first star ship weighed 130,000 tons and was traveling at 13 kilometers per hour. The second star ship weighed 5000 tons and was traveling at 30 kilometers per hour. They collided and the first star ship bounced back so it was traveling at 2 kilometers per hour after the collision. How fast was the second ship traveling?

The ice palace was holding a curling competition. Two of the curlers got out of hand and started hurling their rocks at one another. Their rocks collided head on. The first rock weighed 17 kg and was traveling at 30 meters per second before the collision. After the collision it was traveling in the opposite direction at 25 meters per second. The second rock was traveling at 35 meters per second before the collision and only 20 meters per second after the collision. What was the weight of the second rock?

Elastic Equations Practice Problems
Assume that there is no friction and that the kinetic energy is conserved.

Thomas set two air hockey pucks on the air hockey table, each weighing 50 grams. He sent one flying across the table at 25 meters per second to the left and the other at 10 meters per second to the right so that they collided with one another and bounced straight back. After the collision, the second puck was traveling at 18 meters per second to the left. How fast was the second puck traveling?

$(50)(10) + (50)(-25) = (50)(-18) + (50)(v)$
Remember that you must assign one direction a negative and the other a positive. In the equation above we assigned left the negative and right the positive. You could switch those, but you must remain consistent throughout the problem.
$500 + -1250 = -900 + 50v$
$-750 = -900 + 50v$
$150 = 50v$
$3 = v$

Two star ships were drifting aimlessly toward one another. The first star ship weighed 130,000 tons and was traveling at 13 kilometers per hour. The second star ship weighed 5000 tons and was traveling at 30 kilometers per hour. They collided and the first star ship bounced back so it was traveling at 2 kilometers per hour after the collision. How fast was the second ship traveling?

$(130,000)(13) + (5000)(-30) = (130,000)(-2) + (5000)(v)$
$1,690,000 + -150,000 = -260,000 + 5000v$
$1,540,000 = -260,000 + 5000v$
$1,800,000 = 5000v$
$360 = v$

The ice palace was holding a curling competition. Two of the curlers got out of hand and started hurling their rocks at one another. Their rocks collided head on. The first rock weighed 17 kg and was traveling at 30 meters per second before the collision. After the collision it was traveling in the opposite direction at 25 meters per second. The second rock was traveling at 35 meters per second before the collision and only 20 meters per second after the collision. What was the weight of the second rock?

$(17)(30) + (m)(-35) = (17)(-25) + (m)(20)$
$510 + -35m = -425 + 20m$
$935 = 55m$
$17kg$

Mini Impressionist Gallery

Paint in the style of the Impressionists - a Paris scene, a countryside vista, a seascape, and a picture of the sky.

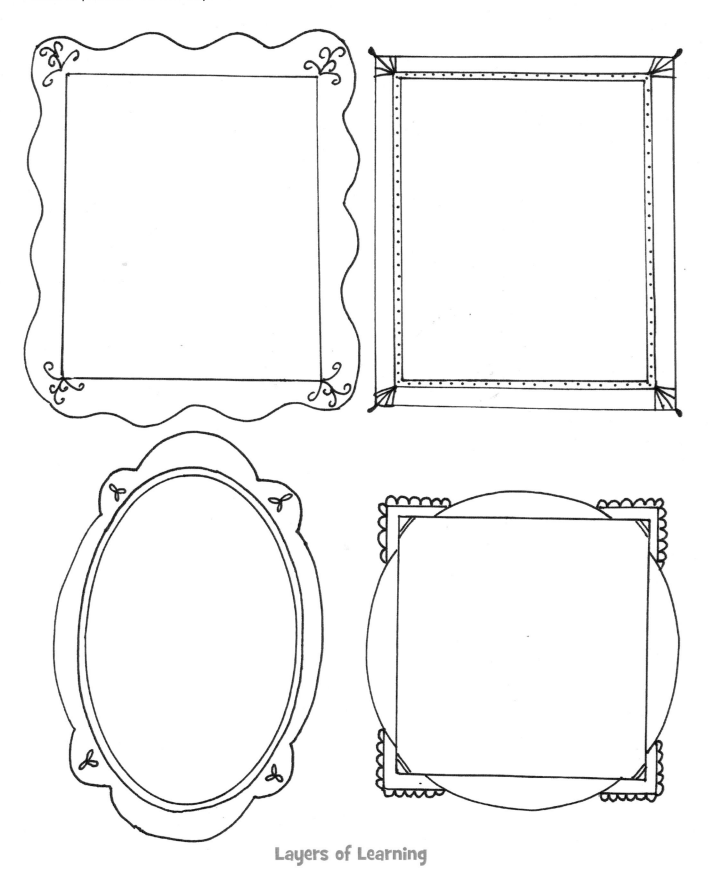

About the Authors

Karen & Michelle . . .
Mothers, sisters, teachers, women who are passionate
about educating kids.
We are dedicated to lifelong learning.

Karen, a mother of four, who has homeschooled her kids for more than
eight years with her husband, Bob, has a bachelor's degree in child de-
velopment with an emphasis in education. She lives in Idaho, gardens,
teaches piano, and plays an excruciating number of board games with
her kids. Karen is our resident arts expert and English guru {most necessary
as Michelle regularly and carelessly mangles the English language and
occasionally steps over the bounds of polite society}.

Michelle and her husband, Cameron, have homeschooled their six boys
for more than a decade. Michelle earned a bachelors in biology, making
her the resident science expert, though she is mocked by her friends for
being the Botanist with the Black Thumb of Death. She also is the go-to for
history and government. She believes in staying up late, hot chocolate,
and a no whining policy. We both pitch in on geography, in case you
were wondering.

Visit our constantly updated blog for tons of free ideas,
free printables, and more cool stuff for sale:
www.Layers-of-Learning.com

Made in the USA
Middletown, DE
04 April 2025

73769533R00038